WELLNESS UNFU*KED

REWRITE YOUR STORY,
RECLAIM YOUR LIFE:
YOUR PRACTICAL GUIDE TO LIFELONG
HAPPINESS AND PURPOSEFUL LIVING

Luke Lintott, M.S.

For seekers of deep, meaningful change in
health, relationships, and self-perception,
*Wellness Unfu*ked* is a practical guide for
lifelong happiness and purposeful living.

CONTENTS

WHY WELLNESS UNFU*KED?

*Wellness Unfu*ked* springs from my own struggles with conventional health standards that often fell short, leaving me yearning for more—more health, love, success, and healing. As a Native American and White, queer, Aquarius ENFP, I used to hide and even oppress the essence of who I am, resulting in challenges with my mental, physical, and spiritual health.

I was born and raised in a conservative small town that clashed with my identities. My home life was similarly difficult, with me growing up amid a storm of divorce, emotional neglect, and challenges related to self-love. My parents divorced when I was six weeks old, and both remarried multiple times. During my parents' heated arguments, I was often the source of their financial and custodial power struggles, which manifested into feelings of insecurity, unlovability, and poor physical and spiritual health.

On top of this, my father figures were homophobic and disdained who I was becoming. They taunted me for how I spoke and expressed myself and told me they were worried I would turn out gay upon entering the sixth grade. And quite unfortunately at the time, I soon realized I was attracted to both men and women.

By the age of 15, I began to cope with these challenges through a combination of alcohol, weed, fad diets, and toxic relationships that I felt I deserved. I struggled with anxiety, insomnia, depression, and a myriad of other challenges that impacted my health, happiness, and overall life fulfillment.

I was fu*ked mentally, physically, and emotionally.

And at one point, I wanted to end it all. But luckily, after breaking down at age 28, I began my *Wellness Unfu*ked* journey.

Through my own trials and tribulations, along with training as a top lifestyle consultant, personal trainer, counselor, and yoga teacher, I created *Wellness Unfu*ked*, which includes a system that aims to get you healthy, wealthy, loved, and healed.

*Wellness Unfu*ked* promises *lifetime* change. It is so much more than another health trend, detox, or mindfulness program. In this book, I give you everything that worked for me and all of the strategies that have transformed my clients' bodies, minds, and lives. By following the steps outlined below, my clients have manifested a healthy body and mind, radical self-love, and their soulmate while *enjoying* the process.

Personally, I used these same steps to get and stay sober for three years after over a decade's struggle with alcohol, to embrace and love my queerness after a lifetime of self-hate, and to get in the best shape of my life while *feeling amazing*.

And this book is so much more than just wellness: I foresee that *Wellness Unfu*ked* will create long-term, global change, resulting in a more harmonious, peaceful, and healthy world.

Remember that how you treat yourself is not only how you treat the world but also how you teach others to treat you.

Are you ready to take the first step? Let's begin! And if you are excited to stay inspired and motivated during your *Wellness Unfu*ked* journey, let's connect on Instagram @limitless_luke and Facebook at https://www. facebook.com/groups/getfitbehappy.

Get comfortable, turn the page, and let's kickstart your *Wellness Unfu*ked* journey toward health, happiness, purpose, love, and boundless healing.

SECTION 1:

COLLECT CLUES - UNDERSTANDING YOUR CURRENT STATE

MY WELLNESS UNFU*KED JOURNEY

"I don't want to be here," I told my therapist as tears began to well up in my eyes. As I hyperventilated, I nervously looked side to side and hunched over into a ball of misery on my black recliner chair. All I could hear was the howling of the wind outside, the thrashing of trees side to side, and the patter of rain against the roof above.

As I looked up, I saw my therapist gaze happily at me through her thick, black glasses. She pulled her brown hair aside and smiled. As I gazed hopelessly to the side, she relaxed into her soft, brown chair as a glimmer of sunlight shined against her pale skin through the 6-inch window above. She was thrilled that I could see clearly now and that I had finally realized I wasn't meant to be a doctor.

But I was devastated.

After six months in medical school, $40,000 more in loans, and lots of misery, I realized that I was climbing the wrong mountain in life. After excelling at all of the pre-med classes required to gain acceptance, quitting a job I loved, and moving across the country, I now realized that medicine would lead to my demise.

This turning point was beyond saddening, as I had given up everyone and everything that brought me happiness to pursue this dream and be what my family and community deemed "successful." I studied more hours than I could count, and my brain hurt from trying to do something that I wasn't naturally good at. Now, all of this turned out to have been wasted energy. I hated doing what I used to think was my life's calling.

I later attended the rest of my medical school classes with a checked-out attitude. People could tell that I didn't care anymore if I got all of the answers right or if my presentation was evidence-based enough for the professor to pass me.

As I walked around the windy, cold, dark streets of Portland, Oregon, that afternoon, I decided my life could not improve. Looking around me, I realized that I no longer saw colors; everything slowly had transformed into a dull black-and-white haze.

I noticed my body was overflowing with rage and betrayal. I betrayed myself when I stopped listening to my inner voice and pursued a career choice that didn't match me. Anger filled my body as I resented those who had told me, "Just do it." I had put far too much emphasis on the advice from my advisors, the normalized feelings of misery among my mentors in the medical field, and my own commitment to proving others wrong.

As I reflected on my failed path, the voices got louder with each creeping minute. I heard my dad criticizing me and telling me that he was worried about me going to medical school and soon laughing at me for dropping out, my own hateful, inner critic telling me I was a loser, and my "friends" rolling their eyes and saying, "I could see that one coming," upon hearing that I left medical school.

That evening, I contemplated killing myself. I walked to a cliff and saw that there were thorns and rocks at the bottom. As I considered ending my life, I thought about my family and friends who would be saddened by my life ending. I remembered that I had studied abroad for a year in Costa Rica and could always move abroad if life in America got too unbearable. And last but not least, I knew that if I jumped, it would likely be a slow and painful death.

At that moment, instead of killing myself, I slowly stepped away from the cliff. And rather than taking my own life, I decided to leave medical school. Within three days of dropping out of medical school, and with little to no time to heal or reflect, I nervously applied to over 150 jobs across the Pacific Northwest. I was so worried about what others would think of my rash decision to drop out of medical school, and so I applied to jobs that looked (but didn't feel) "better" than my failed path at becoming a physician.

After not hearing back from multiple jobs, I decided to lie and say that I lived in Seattle with my then-girlfriend, which was a 6-hour bus ride north. This would increase my likelihood of finding a good-paying job, which I thought would lead others to believe I was "successful." Finally, after being unemployed for a few painful months, I got a temporary job sorting the mail, which would, at the very least, pay the bills as I made this painful transition. But then, a few short months later, things got even worse...

"I don't love you anymore," my girlfriend of nine years told me over the phone as she neared the end of her Bay Area internship. "It's over." Even though our sex life was nearly nonexistent at this time, I was still devastated, as my girlfriend and I had shared our lives and families for so many meaningful years.

And worst of all, she was my dream life partner. She was a short, strong, stocky, beautifully thick Portuguese and Italian girl with thick, curly hair. She had an unparalleled sense of purpose, direction, and confidence.

But although she was my soulmate for so many years, we were now on different wavelengths. While I was struggling to make ends meet, she had made more money at her summer internship at Cisco Systems than I had made in the previous year. And unlike my failed attempts at medical school, my partner was thriving in her Masters in Information Systems program.

While it is true that I could feel a distance when she said she was too busy to talk on the phone during her summer internship in California, I was still in love. In fact, at that moment when she dumped me, I was even debating asking her to marry me.

I then went on to beg her to stay with me. I insisted, "But what will people think? And how will we afford our rent alone?" She went on to explain that she was in a selfish period of her life and didn't love me anymore.

I later met her at the airport when she landed and even attempted to hold her hand as a means to reignite our previous nine years of unconditional love. However, she pulled her hand away from mine and told me she didn't want to lead me to believe we would one day get back together.

She looked at me sadly and muttered, "It's over." Finally, I accepted her words and acknowledged the loss. And consequently, I quickly faded into a deep state of depression.

To cope with my despair, I began getting black-out drunk every weekend. I made sure that my favorite beers would be available for the weekdays in the fridge and guzzled my favorite drink, rum and coke, on the weekends. I loved any event that included bottomless alcohol, ate baked goods like bear claws and donuts for breakfast, and drank copious cups of coffee to stay awake in the morning.

My roommate and I got high on weed every evening. Even though it caused me anxiety and even hallucinations when I did THC-infused edibles, I still smoked weed every evening before bed, as anything was better than being alone. I would show up to my newest job dazed, confused, and hungover. In short order, I found myself drowning in my personal and professional life.

I really didn't care anymore.

Little by little, my body, mind, and skin got worse. The smaller, cute pimples on my face from my early twenties turned into eraser-sized pimples. Every day, I woke up to more blemishes that sometimes popped open and bled onto my pillows during sleep. After trying more skincare regimens than I could count, I gave up on my problematic skin and decided that I would always be unattractive and undesirable.

Simultaneously, as each day wore on, my body got more and more out of shape. Whenever I tried to go to the gym and run, I would begin limping due to knee pain caused by patella femoral syndrome. I decided that it was impossible for someone of my body type to get toned and lean.

Due to my feelings of hopelessness, I gave up on eating a balanced diet and consumed TV dinners, cookies, and old-fashioned glazed donuts on the regular. On top of this, my body hurt from sitting at a desk all day and never stretching. This manifested in me being in a bad, irritated mood most days and lacking energy, zest, and joy.

My negative mindset further manifested in a myriad of digestive issues, gut pain, and horrible gas. My poor digestion and bloating were so bad that I was embarrassed to hang out in big groups, and so I self-isolated even more.

And my solution for all of my ills was the same thing that made me hungover: That oh-so-delicious rum and coke waiting for me in the nearby fridge!

Then suddenly, I entered both the darkest and lightest chapter of my life.

I had just gone to my best friend's wedding with his then-boyfriend in Hawai'i and later spent two magical weeks in Australia, where they lived a joyous life. Upon boarding my plane back to the United States, I decided that I wouldn't live in Seattle forever. Regardless, I was so grateful that I gave myself the gift of 2.5 weeks away from my life, which was my definition of hell on earth.

Little did I know that my wish for drastic change would come in a form I would have never expected.

The day I returned to work after my trip, my boss announced, "Leadership is asking you to quit, and if you don't, we'll terminate you." My heart began beating rapidly, and I began to cry. I asked for a moment to think about it and then went on a long walk to calm my nerves.

I was broken, lost, and hopeless.

As I stared at myself that evening, I hated the person staring back at me in the mirror even more. I despised my unattractive, puffy face. I disliked myself for drinking too much, eating crappy food, and letting myself go. I had lost everything that I cared about, and I blamed myself.

That evening, I couldn't fall asleep. My mind raced about all of the ways my life could go. After finally falling asleep around 4 a.m., I woke up in the morning drained, unfulfilled, and feeling barely alive.

I was completely fu*ked. And after multiple panic attacks and sleepless nights, I finally began listening to my inner voice. I decided to change the trajectory of my body, mind, and life.

Enough was enough. That day, I promised myself that I would never live someone else's dream. I would never do what didn't make me happy. I would never take a job that I abhorred just for the image. I would never pursue a life just because society deemed it "successful" if it clashed with my core values and authentic self.

I decided that I would stop following the status quo.

After seeing my best friends formalize their same-sex partnership, I decided to stop limiting myself. I would begin dating both genders, rather than only women, as I clearly had the capacity to love either.

And yes, I knew that I would let down my family, community, and even my exes when they found out. And that was okay because they weren't living my life.

I decided that I would live a rich, meaningful, and purposeful life. I decided that I would prioritize my health and happiness.

I decided to get unfu*ked.

That evening, I bought a one-way plane ticket to San Diego and applied to jobs that ignited my spirit with joy. Upon landing in my new city with my two checked bags, a martini in my hand, and while eating two fresh cookies in first class (as this was the same price as a coach seat given all of my luggage), I smiled with joy.

I couldn't wait for my new life.

After settling into my new place, I began doing yoga and wellness every day. As I stepped into my new identity, I connected with people who brought me higher. I began to disconnect from the challenging activities, relationships, and beliefs that darkened my essence.

I built deep, authentic bonds with coaches, mentors, and friends both in-person and online. Those first positive connections with other queer individuals blossomed out of dating apps. I later connected with the most amazing souls through yoga, wellness, and other activities that elevated my spirit.

After going down so many roads that fu*ked me up mentally, emotionally, and physically, I did some deep reflection. I connected with my purpose and why I'm here on this planet.

And I began to heal. I healed from my perceived failures of dropping out of medical school. I healed from getting dumped. I healed from the rampant divorce, emotional abuse, and narcissism I survived during my childhood. I healed from being bullied for being queer, Native American, and a pus*y. I healed from suppressing my sexuality to fit in, and I healed from turning to alcohol to cope.

I began to live my dream while pursuing my purpose *and not to feel bad about it.* I found a flow in my love, physical, and business life. I soon founded Luke Yoga and Fitergy after ample inner and outer work, which yielded massive success, happiness, health, and love.

And remember, my *Wellness Unfu*ked* journey wasn't the result of short-lived remedies but a deep, sustainable healing journey. Through hypnosis, energy and nutritional medicine, movement, and so much more, *all of which I've included in this book*, I reprogrammed my body, mind, emotions, and life.

Now, at thirty-six years old, I am beyond happy and healthy, enjoy restful sleep, and am celebrating three years of sobriety after over a decade's struggle with heavy drinking. I embrace my unique essence and celebrate my quirks and queerness. This self-acceptance has had cascade effects in terms of the success of my business, love life, and my now healthy relationship with food, alcohol, myself, and others.

Now, I am paying it forward to you!

Although we have likely not met each other personally, I am so honored to serve as your navigator through **Wellness Unfu*ked: Rewrite Your Story, Reclaim Your Life**.

Get ready for the prime years of your life!

In the following pages, I will walk alongside you as you make the changes to achieve lifelong happiness, purposeful living, and deep, meaningful change in your health, relationships, and self-perception.

But Are You Fu*ked?

Common symptoms of being fu*ked are that you:

- Have a problematic relationship with food, alcohol, scrolling, weed, drugs, porn, or something else.
- Get ghosted by potential partners, dumped by your actual partner, or are sick of being single.

- Notice bad things keep happening to you.
- Feel anxious, angry, or upset about what happened, is happening, or might happen.
- Wake up exhausted, drained, and bored.
- Feel too fat, too skinny, or ugly.
- Dislike, ignore, or abuse your body.
- Don't like the person staring back at you in the mirror.
- Desire direction, health, success, and long-term change in your body, mind, or life.

If any of these resonate with you, you're in the right place. Now, let's refocus on common side effects of unfu*ked wellness…

Let's Get Unfu*ked!

Typical symptoms of unfu*ked wellness are that you:

- Radically love your body, quirks, and personality.
- Are healthy **and** wealthy.
- Get in the best shape of your life.
- Begin dating your dream partner, someone who's beautiful, caring, and has similar life goals.
- Have increased energy, excitement for the future, and enjoyment of this very moment.
- Have the best sex of your entire life.
- Embrace what makes you beautifully you, whether it's your sexuality, sense of humor, or love of feet (*oh yes, you can!*).
- Live a life that's on purpose while attracting meaningful, rich relationships.
- Wake up excited for your day—whether traveling the world, walking in nature, or spending time with high-quality people.

If any of this sounds exciting to you, you're in the right place. And if you desire concrete steps and a system that holds you accountable, I've got you covered!

The CORE Framework is the blueprint for a life of fulfillment, and it serves as the foundation for *Wellness Unfu*ked*. It's used to guide you to recognize your strengths, embrace growth, and achieve your ideal existence:

C – Collect clues about yourself.
O – Opt-in to transformative living.
R – REVITALIZE your entire being.
E – Enjoy the journey of self-rediscovery.

Unpacking unfu*ked wellness, it's clear that mainstream wellness often morphs into an exclusive, oversimplified commodity. Unlike the fleeting, one-size-fits-all solutions, *Wellness Unfu*ked* integrates my comprehensive expertise into a holistic guide for profound healing. Together, we'll ensure that all parts of your true essence heal to the point of unparalleled beauty.

During our time together, we'll explore the four pillars that make up who you are:

- **Mind**: Uncover the secrets to attracting health, love, prosperity, and healing, utilizing hypnosis, the Law of Attraction, breathwork, and proactive measures.
- **Body**: I will show you how to rejuvenate post-trauma, unlocking benefits like weight loss, muscle gain, and vitality.

- **Soul**: Engage in reprogramming to trust your true essence, nurture and parent your inner child, and find true love, leading to purpose, meaningful relationships, wealth, and happiness.
- **Life**: As a premier Lifestyle Consultant & Counselor, I will help you align your existence with your core values, navigate toxic relationships, call in true love, and embrace your boundless potential, ensuring a life of health, affluence, love, and healing.

Self-awareness is key. This book is your interactive guide, offering reflective spaces to help you achieve your goals faster. The effort you invest here will mirror the extraordinary transformation in your body, mind, and life.

For a sustained, fulfilling journey in *Wellness Unfu*ked*, I invite you to engage with our community:

- Follow my suggestions on Instagram @limitless_luke
- Join our encouraging Facebook group at https://www.facebook.com/groups/getfitbehappy
- Let's connect on TikTok @lukelintott
- Enroll in the free *Wellness Unfu*ked* Course for **bonus resources** at: https://wellness.fitergy.co/
- Reach out directly via lukelintott@gmail.com

Let's embrace the journey.

Your *Wellness Unfu*ked* adventure begins now!

UNMASKING YOUR WELLNESS BLUEPRINT

Welcome to what promises to be the journey of a lifetime—a path not just back to wellness but back to your most authentic self. This opening chapter of *Wellness Unfu*ked* serves as your gateway to transformation, a starting point from which you will rediscover and reshape not just your body but your entire life's narrative.

Identifying the Influences on Your Wellness

For many of us, life unfolds on autopilot. We tread paths carved by upbringing and societal norms, rarely questioning the direction or the destination. My journey mirrored this pattern, initially shaped by the conservative values of my small town and the pervasive myths of mainstream wellness. This path led me to a cycle of self-destructive behaviors—intense drinking, extreme diets, and toxic relationships, all underpinned by my struggle with internalized homophobia.

Yet, the pivot came through embracing therapeutic coaching, journaling, hypnosis, and mind-body medicine. I transformed my energy to change my life fundamentally, aligning my actions with my deepest values. This transformation enabled me to attract love, health, wealth, and undeniable success. It propelled me into counseling and led me to establish Fitergy, where wellness is redefined with every executive & corporate wellness consultation offered.

In this chapter, we'll explore the societal and personal influences that have silently shaped your wellness blueprint. True transformation begins the moment you dare confront and question these ingrained beliefs.

It starts with recognizing and dismantling the limiting beliefs that now hold you back.

Join me on this transformative journey with *Wellness Unfu*ked*, where we will begin the foundations of your wellness growth. Together, we will set the stage for a life where you not only pursue your dreams but live them daily, supported by Fitergy's tailored wellness strategies.

Let's embrace this adventure with open hearts and minds and rewrite our stories with health, happiness, and holistic success!

Unpacking Limiting Beliefs and Patterns

As Oprah Winfrey wisely said, "You become what you believe, not what you want." Our beliefs start to form at an early age, often cemented by the age of six. These beliefs can empower us or, as in many cases, create barriers. If you were told you were unlovable or unworthy, these harmful beliefs could hinder your relationships, career, and wellness. They become the invisible chains that restrict our potential.

For instance, being harshly criticized in my own childhood led me to develop crippling perfectionism. I pulled back from opportunities, fearing failure more than embracing growth.

It wasn't until I faced and forgave these past experiences—embracing my imperfections and valuing progress over perfection—that I truly stepped into my power.

Tools for Reflection and Self-Discovery

Embarking on a journey of self-discovery and transformation requires more than just intent—it demands deep reflection and honesty. Now, let's explore structured activities that will shed light on the subconscious beliefs that shape your life.

Here's how we'll tackle these hidden influencers:

Meditative Reflection:

Dedicate time to sit quietly and reflect. Consider the recurring themes and patterns in your life. Ask yourself: What deeply held beliefs might be holding you back? Engaging in this meditative practice is your first step *toward* uncovering these hidden barriers.

Journaling Exercise:

Set a timer and write freely for five minutes about what currently dissatisfies you in your life. Don't censor your thoughts or judge your words; let them flow.

Afterward, look closely at what you've written and reflect on the underlying beliefs that may be driving these feelings.

Circle those beliefs you see repetitively, even if they may now feel gloomy and pessimistic. List out your top 10 negative affirmations so that we can begin reprogramming your mind for success.

The Flip Technique:

Take these negative beliefs you've identified and flip them into powerful, positive affirmations that begin with "I am," "I have," "I attract," "I see," or another form that begins with "I..."

For example, if you frequently think, "I am not good enough," flip this and write down your affirmation, "I am good enough." Or transform "I am ugly and unattractive" to "I am beautiful" or "I choose to believe I am beautiful."

Now, you get to create new beliefs that feel good, are realistic and specific, and reflect who you're becoming and what you're attracting.

Your affirmations should be positive and focus on your desires rather than what you want to avoid, don't have, or don't enjoy.

Remember that simple, succinct affirmations are powerful tools for reprogramming your subconscious mind. They are more easily understood and accepted by your subconscious childhood brain.

As an example, here are the Unfu*ked Affirmations for Julia, a life coach who is calling in her soulmate, new clients, and love:

1) I have sexy curves.
2) I am a succinct, eloquent communicator.
3) I value myself.
4) I have an abundance of money.
5) I love myself unconditionally.
6) I am pretty.
7) I am strong.
8) I am confident.
9) I am good enough.
10) I magnetize money.

Now it's your turn! Apply this same technique to create your first 10 affirmations on the U*nfu*ked Affirmations Worksheet* in the appendices, which will serve as the foundation for your *Wellness Unfu*ked* journey.

After writing down all of your affirmations, verbally record them on your device while you're in a high-vibe state. Every day after waking up, listen to your unfu*ked affirmations while you're getting ready for your day.

This simple but powerful action will help raise your frequency as you begin your day right, magnetizing loving relationships, health, wealth, success, and boundless healing.

Visualize and Affirm Daily:

Write your top affirmations on sticky notes and place them in locations where you will see them every day—like your bathroom mirror, your computer monitor, or your refrigerator. Start with affirmations like, "I love myself unconditionally" or "I am open to challenging myself to be better." These visible reminders will serve as daily cues to reinforce your new mindset, supporting your journey to a fully unfu*ked wellness.

By engaging in these practices, you lay the groundwork for significant personal growth. You're not just dreaming of a better life; you're actively rewriting your script to achieve it. Use these tools to peel back the layers of past conditioning and step into the empowered version of yourself. Remember, every affirmation you see and repeat is not just a statement but a stepping stone *toward* realizing your deepest desires and your most authentic self.

CHAPTER 3

THE WELLNESS AUDIT - ASSESSING YOUR STARTING POINT

With the newfound awareness gained from Chapter 2, you are now prepared to dive deeper into your self-assessment. The Wellness Audit is not just an evaluation—it's a foundational step toward building a resilient and fulfilled life.

Conducting a Comprehensive Self-Assessment

"Reflection is one of the most underused yet powerful tools of success,"
– Richard Carlson

Before deciding what you desire, it's critical to evaluate where you stand. Self-awareness and reflection build the foundation for your *Wellness Unfu*ked* journey and empower you to become happier, healthier, and more successful in your personal and professional pursuits.

In this phase, we evaluate the four pillars of you: Mind, Body, Spirit, and Life. This holistic approach ensures that no aspect of your wellness is overlooked. Using a simple scale from 1 to 10, you'll gauge your current state in each area and explore the reasons behind these ratings.

Try This: Evaluate the 4 Pillars of You!

Overall evaluation of the 4 Pillars of You from 1 (worst) to 10 (best):
- Mind:
- Body:
- Spirit:
- Life:

Why did you choose this number?
- Mind:
- Body:
- Spirit:
- Life:

What causes you to stay here?
- Mind:
- Body:
- Spirit:
- Life:

What would bring you higher?
- Mind:
- Body:
- Spirit:
- Life:

Reflection questions:
1. **What pillar(s) are your strengths? Why?**
2. **What pillar(s) are your areas of growth? Why?**
3. **What steps will you take this week to improve your areas of growth?**
4. **What would make you feel successful in the next 365 days?**

Creating Your Wellness Audit Report

"Nothing is impossible to the person who backs desire with enduring faith." – Napoleon Hill

Welcome to a pivotal section of *Wellness Unfu*ked*, where we dive into creating your Wellness Audit Report. This transformative tool will guide you through the next 365 days.

Here, you will clarify what you truly desire, envision what achieving these desires looks like, and identify any obstacles that might stand in your way. This comprehensive exploration will reveal potential blind spots that have previously hindered your progress.

Furthermore, this exercise will serve as a foundation for the intentional actions you'll take throughout the coming year.

Articulate Your Desires and Outline Your Path

This report acts as your personal roadmap, detailing your ambitions for the next year and breaking them down into manageable, insightful components. It's designed to help you articulate and focus on what you truly want to achieve rather than those values that society or others may have placed upon you.

Additionally, this report highlights your strengths and addresses areas that will need growth, love, and care during your wellness journey.

Try This: Journal What You Desire in the Next 365 Days

Today's Date:

What do you desire in the next 365 days?
- Mind:
- Body:
- Spirit:
- Life:

What are signs that this desire has been completed?
- Mind:
- Body:
- Spirit:
- Life:

What are the desired side effects of completing this goal (e.g. your soulmate, increased income, joy, etc.)?
- Mind:
- Body:
- Spirit:
- Life:

Creative expression: Draw what your body, mind, spirit, and life would look like when the numbers above are at your ideal level.

Mapping Out Success: The ASK Methodology

As you outline your desires, consider the three critical keys to successful behavior change: Attitude, Skills, and Knowledge (ASK). Each element is vital in setting goals and creating a plan of action.

When your attitudes, skills, and knowledge related to your goal are strong, you are more likely to make a behavior change, which ensures long-term change and aids you in getting into flow, where success meets no resistance.

Keep in mind that if one of the keys to behavior change (attitude, skills or knowledge) is lacking, you're unlikely to be successful at accomplishing your goals. For instance, if you desire to get toned and lean but have a negative, hopeless attitude towards movement and improving your diet, it matters little if you have both the skills and knowledge to accomplish your fitness goals.

Luckily, there is hope! Through taking the steps below, you will illuminate your strengths and areas of growth, and create actionable steps to make permanent behavior changes possible. Example actions include joining a coaching program, doing some research online, or even something simple such as fine-tuning your cooking skills.

Now, let's begin! Reflect on these areas to ensure no component is lacking, as any deficit can potentially derail your progress.

Try This: Evaluate the Three Critical Keys to Behavior Change: The ASK Methodology

Your Top Goal:

Self-assessment of your attitude from 1 (Negative, pessimistic) to 10 (Positive, optimistic, supportive):
- Why?
- What would increase this number?

Self-assessment of your skills from 1 (you don't have the skills to do what is needed to manifest my desires) to 10 (you have the ability to do what I desire):
- Why?
- What would increase this number?

Self-assessment of your knowledge from 1 (you are unsure what to do) to 10 (you know what steps to take):
- Why?
- What would increase this number?

ASK Reflection:
- What are your strengths?
- What are your areas of growth?
- What actions could propel you to the next level in the coming year?

By methodically assessing these elements, you equip yourself with a clear understanding of where you stand and what you need to move forward. The goal in creating this Wellness Audit Report isn't just to set goals; it's about transforming them into tangible results that will enrich your life in every aspect.

This is your moment to step boldly *toward* a year of unprecedented growth and fulfillment. Let's make your desires a reality!

Letter From My 120-Year-Old Self

To conclude this section, I invite you to engage in a powerful visualization exercise. Imagine a conversation with your 120-year-old self, who is now happily on their deathbed and has lived a full, vibrant life.

Envision that everything in your life went far better than expected. At the end of your life, your future self is guiding you, cheering you on, and sharing how wonderful your life was through a letter that they write to their former self.

Write a letter from this wise, future self to your present self. Make this a letter from your future self filled with wisdom, gratitude, and insights from a well-lived life.

Include ample details in this letter that illustrate the wonderful relationships, love, health, comfort, freedom, success, and time that you enjoyed while on this earthly plane.

Craft your letter in a loving, uplifting, and grateful tone, as you are now the most expressed version of yourself at the most advanced time in your amazing life.

Give yourself advice on what to truly value, and share insights into what helps you live a happy, purposeful life.

Identify the light, beauty, and strength that result from challenges you may face during your lifespan. Share positive affirmations, words of encouragement, and insights for your time on this planet.

Close your eyes now and envision that you are connecting with your future 120-year-old self. Inhale and exhale.

After reflecting, use the *Letter From My 120-Year-Old Self* Worksheet in the Appendices to outline your letter from your future self. Next, verbally record this letter with enthusiasm into your device.

Every morning after waking up, listen to the recording of your letter, along with your first ten unfu*ked affirmations.

Listening to these positive words, no matter where you are or what you're doing, ensures that your highest self guides you *toward* your desires.

Remember that this Wellness Audit is the first step in a series of actions that will lead you *toward* getting your wellness unfu*ked.

Share your goals and this letter with someone you trust—be it a mentor, friend, or coach. This act of sharing not only affirms your commitment but also starts building a supportive community around your vision.

As we move forward in *Wellness Unfu*ked*, remember that each step aims not just to challenge you but to champion you *toward* self-discovery and true fulfillment. You are not alone on this journey; together, we will rewrite your story and reclaim your life, ensuring that each chapter that follows is even more empowering.

Ready to embark on this transformative journey? Turn the page, and let's continue to unfu*k your wellness, unlocking limitless happiness, health, love, wealth, and success.

This is just the beginning of your new, unscripted adventure *toward* a fulfilled, purposeful life.

SECTION 2:

OPT-IN TO TRANSFORMATIVE LIVING - SETTING INTENTIONS FOR TRANSFORMATION

Welcome to the heartbeat of your transformation—where you opt-in to a journey that is uniquely yours. In this section, we'll harness the power of intention to fuel your passage through the CORE Framework for Life Fulfillment.

Through hypnosis, visualization, and creating goals that are in complete alignment, you'll commit to the life you've always wanted but perhaps never dared to fully pursue.

CHAPTER 4

FU*K THE FEAR - EMBRACING CHANGE

"Change begins at the end of your comfort zone." – Roy T. Bennett

Change isn't just necessary; it's life itself.

But embracing it requires overcoming the instinctive fears that have safeguarded humans for millennia. Fear was especially in the past—when we were living in the wild and were unsure about where we would get our next meal. It helped us avoid losing our lives while fighting our predators or gathering resources for our family to avoid starvation.

However, for most of us, our needs are now met, and fear actually causes more problems than solutions. This fear and ignoring the bigger picture can sometimes cripple us from taking action.

As an example, think of a frog in slowly boiling water. As the water gently heats up, the frog typically dies a slow and painful death, unaware—and sometimes ignoring—that drastic change is necessary to survive.

This metaphor is a stark reminder that if we don't act decisively and make changes even when it's uncomfortable or when we are afraid, we risk experiencing a long, agonizing end.

In other words, it's time to jump out of the soon-to-be boiling water!

My pivotal moment came during the global pause of COVID-19, when I transitioned from yoga studios to virtual classes, just seven days after my yoga studio furloughed me.

This decision required a complete reinvention of myself, and it taught me that when change is the only option, embracing it can open doors you never knew existed. Even greater shifts have happened through making decisive changes and stepping through the fear *even when it isn't currently necessary to merely survive.*

Side effects of such intentional actions include wonderful relationships, bountiful happiness, amazing health, and long-term success.

Now, let's embrace change and conquer our fears together!

Try This: Embrace Change Through Intentional Action.

- **Identify Your Challenges:** What are the biggest obstacles you're currently facing? Understand them clearly to navigate effectively.
- **Motivation for Change:** Why is this change essential? Link your reasons to deep personal values and the outcomes you desire. If you're still feeling stuck, answer the following questions to increase motivation:
    - Why am I motivated to make the change?
    - If I don't make a change, what will my life look like in the future if things stay the same?
    - What would my life look like if things got worse?
    - What would keep me committed to my goals?

> - **Visualize Outcomes:** What does the status quo look like versus a transformed future? Imagine both scenarios in detail to create a sense of urgency and clarity. Visualize your desires consistently and frequently to attract your desires sooner.

Conquering Fear and Embracing Uncertainty

Fear, while once a crucial survival mechanism for our ancestors, now often serves as a barrier that blocks us from achieving our fullest potential. To transcend these fears, we begin by laying them bare.

Mapping Out Your Fears:

Today, I encourage you to write down your greatest fears. This simple act can demystify them and diminish their control over you. Once they're on paper, they're not looming as large in your mind.

Creating Your Battle Plan:

With your fears in front of you, start scripting out specific strategies to navigate and overcome potential setbacks. This proactive approach not only prepares you for challenges but also empowers you to move forward despite the fear.

Facing Fear with Courage:

Acknowledging your fear is a brave first step *toward* mastery over it. For years, I let my fears of launching my wellness business and pursuing my master's degree stop me from taking action. Only after actually writing down the worst-case scenario did I strip away the power of my fears and take action *toward* my desires.

Now it's your turn! Engage with these probing questions to deepen your understanding and readiness:

Try This: Face Your Fears with Courage!

1. **What is the worst-case scenario?** Visualize the absolute toughest outcome.
2. **How would you handle that scenario?** Imagine yourself managing this situation successfully.
3. **Who's got your back?** Identify the support network that will stand by you if things go south.
4. **What proactive steps can you take to prevent the worst but still advance boldly?**

By answering these questions, you not only prepare yourself for the realities of risks but also reinforce your resilience. Fear acknowledged is fear half-conquered. So, let's take that bold step forward with a plan in hand and a heart ready to face the uncertainties with confidence.

Let this journey redefine not just the boundaries of your comfort zone but expand the horizons of your capabilities.

Unfu*ked Visualization Script

Now, let's dive into creating your Unfu*ked Visualization Script, which you can find in the appendices. This script is your blueprint for the next 365 days, and we will develop one with rich descriptions and vivid imagery that brings your ideal future to life.

Visualization & the Law of Expectation

Your mind is a powerful ally. About 90-95% of your brain activity happens subconsciously, with your brain unable to distinguish between vivid imagination and reality. When you consistently visualize your dream scenario, you align your emotions and vibrations with the life you want to manifest.

The Law of Expectation supports this, suggesting that what you anticipate with certainty tends to materialize. Dr. Milton Erickson, a renowned hypnotherapist, first identified the Law of Expectation, which estimates that 85% of what you expect will happen.

This is similar to the well-documented placebo effect, where belief alone can manifest physical changes and improvements.

Remember that the Law of Expectation does not play favorites, meaning that both your negative and positive expectations are destined to happen. As such, if you expect bad things to happen, undesirable experiences may come your way, even if you hope for the exact opposite.

Your belief system, which is typically cemented during childhood, influences your expectations. This can be good or bad. If you were raised to believe that the world is a scary place and that you can't accomplish your dreams, this will similarly limit your potential no matter what actions you take.

If you feel that negative expectations and a misaligned belief system are still holding back, there is hope. You can transform your expectations and reprogram your subconscious mind for your success now as an adult!

And when the critical step of visualization and positive expectations is paired with aligned action, your manifesting abilities explode! Personally, I took these same steps outlined below to go from crippling self-doubt and insecurity to expecting the best-case scenario and calling in dream clients, love, health, happiness, and success.

Now it's your turn. Let's call in your dreams consistently and regularly through your Unfu*ked Visualization Script!

Creating Your Future:

Using the *Unfu*ked Visualization Script* worksheet in the appendices, start your script with the words, "I am so excited..." and paint a detailed picture of everything you desire. Describe the wonderful emotions, the settings, the sounds, and even the scents that accompany your vision.

Make your visualization your own, and filled with juicy descriptions, lots of positive feelings, and affirmations that help you feel good.

Ensure that your *Unfu*ked Visualization Script* is thrilling yet believable.

As a source of inspiration, I've included an example of the Unfu*ked Visualization Script for Joey, the Wellness Entrepreneur who is calling in financial abundance and his dream partner:

My Unfu*ked Visualization Script: I am so excited to have $88,000 and will be making plans to move into my own condo that has 2 bedrooms. I will also purchase a beautiful new car in cash. I will have begun a retirement that includes regular additions to it. I will also offer to pay for dinner when we go out to eat with my family and friends. I am so happy and fulfilled. I am abundant. Abundance surrounds me right now!

I will be seriously dating my soulmate, who is a famous, charismatic business owner. He is handsome and kind, and is also living his purpose. He will adore me and look up to me, but also push me to be better. He will accelerate my career by being real with me, and encouraging me to keep going even when times get tough. We will be excitedly preparing for our upcoming wedding in the fall.

Daily Reinforcement:

Record this script on your device and make it part of your morning routine. Listening to it daily will not only inspire you but also prime you for actions most aligned with your goals.

The Power of Hypnosis:

As Dr. Joe Dispenza famously said, "When you change your energy, you change your life." Hypnosis is a transformative tool for deepening this change, enabling massive shifts in your beliefs and emotions, which are the foundation of your actions.

Before integrating hypnosis into my routine, I sabotaged my own success, heavily drank alcohol, and disliked myself despite ample mindset work.

Thankfully, hypnosis was the key that unlocked my self-acceptance, catalyzed my sobriety, and transformed my self-image from negative to empowered.

How Hypnosis Works:

In a hypnotic state, your brain operates in theta waves, a deeply meditative state where you remain aware yet open to new possibilities. This state allows direct communication with your subconscious, helping to overwrite outdated scripts with new, empowering narratives.

Integrating Hypnosis into Your Routine:

Incorporate hypnosis into your daily regimen, ideally during the twilight hours, either just before you sleep or right after you wake up when your subconscious is most receptive.

Starting Your Hypnosis Journey:

1. **Find a Calm Space:** Choose a quiet area where you can relax without interruptions.
2. **Physical Relaxation:** Lie down or sit comfortably, take deep breaths, and methodically relax ten specific parts of your body.
3. **Mental Calmness:** Slowly count down from ten to one, deepening your state of relaxation with each number.
4. **Visualize:** Spend a few minutes immersed in the vivid details of your Unfu*ked Visualization Script.
5. **Affirmations:** Introduce your affirmations, feeling each one as though it's already your reality.
6. **Return:** Gently count yourself back to full awareness, feeling refreshed and aligned.

For an easy start, tap into my guided hypnosis session available on the *Wellness Unfu*ked* Course website at <u>wellness.fitergy.co</u>

This tool is your gateway to transforming your deepest beliefs and stepping into the life you've always imagined.

Embrace this transformative journey with the *Unfu*ked Visualization Script* and see how hypnosis can lead you to a life unfettered by past limitations.

Here's to becoming unfu*ked in all the best ways!

CHAPTER 5

DEFINE YOUR VISION – DESIGNING YOUR IDEAL LIFE

Now, you are ready to define the vision of your ultimate life. This framework is designed to help you make monumental changes that align with your deepest purposes.

Before I took these same steps, I pursued jobs, relationships, and wellness activities that didn't match me at my core. This led to heightened levels of anxiety, stress, and burnout.

Luckily, upon connecting deeply with what makes my heart sing, I've called in such wonderful experiences, relationships, health, and self-love.

Now, let's begin planning for your dream life!

Creating Your Future:

1. **Life Alignment**: Before setting out your vision, you must connect deeply with your purpose. This connection diminishes dependence on external validation and fortifies your resilience against challenges.
2. **Dream Big:** What would you do if limitations were lifted? Imagine your life with no constraints—where would you live, who would be by your side, how would you feel every day?
3. **Visualization and Goal Setting:** Utilize the power of your subconscious, which doesn't differentiate between real and

vividly imagined experiences. Spend time daily visualizing your dream life, enhancing this with a **vision board** that acts as a constant reminder of your goals.

Creating a Manifestation Calendar

As you continue on this beautiful journey of self-discovery and achievement, I want to introduce a powerful tool that will not only inspire but also organize your path to greatness: the Manifestation Calendar.

We are going to use this roadmap to chart the course to your future joy and fulfillment!

Here's how you can create a Manifestation Calendar that vibrates with energy and intention:

1. **Visualize and Strategize**: Start by envisioning where you want to be in the next year. What milestones will mark significant progress *toward* your dreams? Identify 2-3 key achievements for each month that align with your ultimate goals. These should be stepping stones to your greater vision.

2. **Celebrate Your Progress**: Before you look forward, take a moment to reflect back. Create a retrospective of the previous twelve months on your calendar. Highlight all that you've accomplished, big and small. This exercise isn't just about patting yourself on the back—it's about recognizing the power you have to manifest your reality and building momentum as you realize how far you've come.

3. **Daily Inspiration**: Place your vision board and Manifestation Calendar somewhere you will see them every day. Set this visual reminder as the wallpaper of your smartphone, tablet, and other devices, or place a physical copy of it in your car, room, or

bathroom. This visual reminder of where you've been and where you're headed will serve as a daily source of inspiration. Each time you glance at your calendar or vision board, allow yourself to feel good now. It's this positive vibration that will attract your desires sooner and inspire you to take aligned action every day.

By actively engaging with your Manifestation Calendar, you do more than just plan—you invite the energy of anticipation, celebration, and action into your daily life. Let this calendar be a testament to what you can achieve and a beacon that guides you through the days ahead.

Here's to manifesting a future brimming with success and satisfaction!

Goal Setting: Your Pathway to a Fulfilling Future

Tony Robbins once said, "Most people overestimate what they can do in a year and underestimate what they can do in two or three decades." This point is a powerful reminder of the importance of setting goals that are not only ambitious but also aligned with our life's purpose and long-term vision.

Here's how you can set goals that keep you motivated, accountable, and on track to achieving your deepest desires:

1. **Align with Your Purpose**: First and foremost, ensure that your goals are in harmony with your life's purpose. This alignment is crucial as it ensures that every step you take is not just a move *toward* achieving a goal but a stride *toward* fulfilling your destiny.
2. **Write It Down**: Research shows that writing down your goals increases your likelihood of achieving them by a staggering 90%. By putting your goals on paper, you make them tangible and set in motion the process of manifestation.

3. **Set SMART Goals**: Focus on creating goals that are Specific, Measurable, Achievable, Relevant, and Time-bound. These criteria transform vague ambitions into clear, actionable pathways.

4. **Balance Ambition with Enjoyment**: While it's important to challenge yourself, it's equally critical to ensure that your goals are enjoyable. This balance keeps the journey gratifying and sustainable. Spend the majority of your time operating within your "zone of genius"—the activities that you are not only good at but that also energize you, ensuring that your journey *toward* your goals remains a joyful one.

5. **Break It Down**: Structuring your goals across different time frames can provide you with short-term targets and long-term visions:

    - Weekly Goals: What small steps can you take this week that will build the foundation for your larger goals?
    - Monthly Goals: Identify larger milestones you can realistically achieve within a month that will contribute to your annual goals.
    - Annual Goals: Set significant objectives that will mark substantial progress *toward* your decade-long aspirations.
    - Decade Goals: Define where you want to be in ten years. How do these goals align with your ultimate life purpose?
    - 20-Year Goals: Dream big—where do you see yourself in twenty years? How do these visions align with your life's purpose and the legacy you wish to leave?

6. **Celebrate and Adjust**: As you achieve each milestone, take the time to celebrate your success. This not only affirms your progress but also boosts your morale. Be prepared to adjust your goals as needed—flexibility is key to accommodating the unpredictable nature of life while keeping your core objectives in focus.

By setting goals that are aligned with your deepest desires and breaking them down into manageable steps, you empower yourself to not only dream big but also to achieve big. Let each goal be a stepping stone *toward* a future where you live your purpose fully and joyfully.

Here's to setting goals that inspire you to rise, shine, and thrive in every aspect of your life!

To ensure long-term success, fulfillment, and joy, it's essential to set your goals holistically, covering all aspects of your being. Use the table below to set your goals within the 4 Pillars of You: mind, body, spirit, and life. This holistic approach ensures that each part of you is aligned and thriving, contributing to a balanced and joyful journey *toward* your ultimate aspirations.

Try This: Write Down Your SMART Goals.

What are your SMART goals for the next week?
- Mind:
- Body:
- Spirit:
- Life:

What are your SMART goals for the next month?
- Mind:
- Body:
- Spirit:
- Life:

What are your SMART goals for the next year?
- Mind:
- Body:
- Spirit:
- Life:

What are your SMART goals for the next 10 years?
- Mind:
- Body:
- Spirit:
- Life:

What are your SMART goals for the next 20 years?
- Mind:
- Body:
- Spirit:
- Life:

CHAPTER 6

COMMITMENT AND ACCOUNTABILITY - YOUR WELLNESS CONTRACT

Commitment to wellness is much like signing a pact with your future self, a promise to pursue a life marked not just by temporary wins but by deep, meaningful transformation. Here in this chapter, you'll be engaging in actively creating your very own Wellness Contract.

This is your chance to define and chase what "success" really looks like in your most fulfilled life while understanding more clearly who and what holds you accountable.

Wellness isn't a destination but a vibrant, evolving journey. It's not about hitting a number on the scale, reaching a financial milestone, or finding a partner—it's about the enduring, day-to-day process that enriches your existence in every aspect.

You've already begun this journey with tools like your unfu*ked affirmations, your unfu*ked visualization script, and your transformative daily hypnosis routine. These aren't just steps on a path; they are the path.

Each breath, each affirmation, and each session of hypnosis is a victory in itself.

But let's deepen that commitment. It's time to draft a Wellness Contract—a heartfelt commitment to yourself. The goal of this is to embed daily actions that align with your core values and long-term objectives, actions that will propel you forward regardless of the immediate outcomes.

Creating Your Wellness Contract

In your contract, focus on the process, not just outcomes. Specify at least three daily or weekly actions that represent your commitment to wellness, such as completing this book, practicing hypnosis daily, and starting each day with your personalized affirmations.

Now, consider the broader spectrum of your life:

Plan Your Ideal Week:

Sketch out your perfect week, where every activity enriches your well-being. This plan should mirror your values and long-term goals.

Try This: Plan Your Ideal Week

Sketch out your perfect week, where every activity enriches your well-being. This plan should mirror your values and long-term goals.

What is your ideal Monday?
- Morning:
- Mid-Day:
- Evening:

What is your ideal Tuesday?
- Morning:
- Mid-Day:
- Evening:

What is your ideal Wednesday?

- Morning:
- Mid-Day:
- Evening:

What is your ideal Thursday?

- Morning:
- Mid-Day:
- Evening:

What is your ideal Friday?

- Morning:
- Mid-Day:
- Evening:

What is your ideal Saturday?

- Morning:
- Mid-Day:
- Evening:

What is your ideal Sunday?

- Morning:
- Mid-Day:
- Evening:

If you struggle to fit key activities into your week, ask yourself why. Is your current job or relationship supporting your wellness, or is it a barrier? What changes could make your environment more conducive to your wellness goals?

Build Your Support Network:

Oprah Winfrey wisely advised, "Surround yourself only with people who will lift you higher." As you continue your *Wellness Unfu*ked* journey, the company you keep can either anchor you back or propel you forward.

When I went down a pathway of self-destruction, I stayed closely connected with people who weren't rooting for my rise and those who didn't love who I truly was. I watered down who I was and even changed my core values to be liked, loved, and followed.

Things dramatically improved when I distanced myself from people who drained the essence of who I am and identified those individuals who embraced who I'm becoming.

If there is someone out there who brings you higher and has many of the facets of who you're becoming, it's valuable to follow those individuals and spend quality time with them. You become who you surround yourself with, and so it's similarly essential to surround yourself with people who love who you are and bring you higher.

Detail Your Support System:

List down the people who genuinely support your *Wellness Unfu*ked* journey. Rate each on how well they help you *toward* your goals, and reflect on why they are effective or otherwise.

Name:

Support Rating (1-10):

Why?

Name:

Why?

Support Rating (1-10):

Name:

Why?

Support Rating (1-10):

Consider how these individuals contribute to your wellness. Do they encourage you? Do they challenge you to be better? What might be holding them back from fully supporting you?

Join a Community:

Expand your network by connecting with like-minded individuals. Join communities like our "Mindfully Sculpted" group on Facebook, where daily motivation and support are abundant. Connect with coaches, mentors, friends, and organizations that elevate your spirits and support your *Wellness Unfu*ked* journey.

Simultaneously, distance yourself from those relationships that are no longer aligned with who you are becoming. Unfollow and/or mute online accounts that no longer resonate with the new you, and step away from in-person relationships that make you feel more drained than uplifted.

This chapter is all about taking action. By setting these commitments, you're not just aspiring to change; you're doing it. Engage with us, share your journey, and let's thrive together.

Your path to deep, meaningful wellness starts here. Embrace it, commit to it, and watch as your life transforms!

SECTION 3:

REVITALIZE YOUR BODY - THE PHYSICAL PILLAR

UNLEASH YOUR INNER WELLNESS WARRIOR

Welcome to the transformative journey of connecting your mind with your body—this is where we unleash your inner Wellness Warrior. Despite having a seemingly perfect regimen—exercising, eating right, and pampering my skin—I struggled with the disconnection between my body and mind, fueled by past regrets and unkind self-talk.

It wasn't until I faced some of my life's toughest moments—losing my job and a long-term relationship and a stint living in my parents' basement—that I found the pathway to true self-acceptance and profound self-love.

This chapter guides you to nurturing a positive body image and cultivating a deep, loving connection with yourself.

Now, let's begin creating your foundation for physical and mental revitalization!

Exploring the Mind-Body Connection:
Start with reflection. Our bodies listen to everything our minds say. I learned this the hard way, speaking to myself harshly and treating my body as an enemy rather than an ally.

Everything changed when I shifted to nurturing thoughts and began treating myself with kindness and compassion. Here's how you can start:

- Reflect on your journey: What challenges have you overcome? How have these experiences made you stronger?
- Journal your self-love: What do you admire about your body? Why are you grateful for it? What positive changes are you excited to make?

Your Subconscious Superpower

Your body is in your mind.

Your mindset, both positive and negative, manifests in your physical form. That's why people who feel negatively about themselves often have higher rates of anxiety and stress, which can make it difficult to get quality sleep, eat the right foods, and exercise regularly.

Furthermore, adverse feelings also affect your gene expression, which can literally activate the onset of disease. That's why people with a negative mindset often have higher rates of addiction, cancer, and even chronic diseases like heart disease.

Adverse emotions and beliefs can also increase the release of the stress hormone cortisol, which can cause you to lose or gain weight.

Without a doubt, creating a body transformation is so much more than taking action alone!

To make transformational, lifetime changes to your physical form, it is essential to reprogram your thoughts, emotions, and beliefs. When you think positively, and your beliefs align with the body you're building, you're more likely to be successful at accomplishing your fitness goals, feel good about the positive changes you're making, and continue forward even when life throws you curveballs.

To begin your fitness goals right, begin by surrounding yourself with people, activities, and places that lift you higher, help you feel good now, and support you on your fitness goals. This could mean spending more time in nature, calling up a friend to take a yoga class with you, and following people online that lift your spirits. Similarly, it may be helpful during this time to distance yourself from those people, places, and activities that may sabotage your wellness goals.

To tap into your best self, create affirmations that resonate with your wellness journey *toward* self-love, resilience, and your desired body and mind. Write these affirmations starting with "I am…" and place them somewhere you will see them daily. Here are a few to consider:

- I am toned, muscular, and lean.
- I am strong.
- I am worthy of respect and love from myself and others.

Add these newest beliefs to your Unfu*ked Affirmations Worksheet. Record these affirmations into your device, and listen to them while getting ready for your day. Last but not least, place your affirmations into your subconscious using the power of hypnosis during the twilight hours before bed or upon rising.

Filling Your Self-Care Cup:

As you prepare to make changes that support your physical form, it's important to do things that feel good now and align with your healthiest, most loved self.

First, think about what fills your self-care cup. These are the activities that restore your energy and make you feel whole. Whether it's yoga, meditation, or dancing in your living room, identify what uplifts you and commit to these practices regularly. Create a list that you can turn to, ensuring you have a toolset ready for both the highs and lows of life.

Next, make a list of those activities or things that you can give yourself as rewards for taking actions that align with your fitness goals. For some people, this may mean giving yourself a massage every two weeks after completing your goal of five workouts per week. Remember that these gifts align with who you are becoming and are things that your future self would love doing or receiving on the regular.

Pick things that both feel good and support, rather than sabotage, your fitness goal. Instead of rewarding yourself for adding in cardio five times per week with ice cream, alcohol, or scrolling, identify a self-care activity that aligns with your future self. This could instead be a facial, a trip to the beach, or even a cup of coffee or tea at your favorite local cafe.

Now, let's begin! Write self-care cup gifts for easy reference as you reward yourself for making changes, which will, in turn, speed up your *Wellness Unfu*ked* journey.

My Self-Care Cup Gifts:

1)

2)

3)

4)

5)

CHAPTER 8

NOURISH AND THRIVE - OPTIMAL NUTRITION AND EXERCISE

Before I properly fueled and moved my body, I felt like sh*t. But luckily, I began feeling and looking amazing when I took action to support my body transformation, even before I was ready!

For me, this meant:

- Showing up to yoga and fitness classes alone, even when it felt awkward and unfamiliar.
- Making minor pivots to my diet and hydration routine, which created massive changes in my body, skin, and life.
- Releasing alcohol completely from my diet after realizing that drinking less just didn't work.

In this part of your *Wellness Unfu*ked* journey, you get to customize your exercise and nutrition routine for optimal health. Side effects of taking action include toned, lean muscle, strong bones, and a healthy body and mind.

And remember, eating well and exercising aren't just about looking good— they're about feeling amazing and empowering your life on multiple levels. From improving your love life to enhancing your connection with the universe, the right nutrition and fitness regimen can transform more than just your physique; they can elevate your entire existence.

In this section, I'm giving you everything that has worked for both myself and my clients to get in the best shape of your life.

And the universe has your back!

I'm cheering for you as you invest in the most valuable thing that you have—your health. You got this!

Now, are you ready?

Let's now begin your *Wellness Unfu*ked* body transformation.

Creating a Balanced Nutrition Plan:
Eating the right foods helps you increase your energy, grow muscle, and burn fat. However, even if you follow the nutrition plan I've crafted for you below while still binging on problematic foods and beverages on the side, this will sabotage your success.

That's why the first step in transforming how you fuel your body is to altogether remove those foods and beverages that cause you to binge. For sugar addicts, this means throwing away all cookies, candies, and sodas. For heavy drinkers, this means giving away all spirits, beers, and alcoholic beverages to one of your drinking friends and tossing out old bottles and cans. And if you know that cannabis or other substances cause you to binge, it's crucial to discard or give away these items as well.

Now, if you're not ready to completely release these foods and substances, at the very least, reorganize your kitchen so that these items are unseen and challenging to access. This could mean putting that bag of chips in the top cupboard that is only accessible with a step stool or stashing your bread in the freezer where it is less easy to consume when cravings hit.

Now that you've eliminated and avoided those substances that may cause you to self-sabotage, let's create the foundation for your *Wellness Unfu*ked* nutrition battle plan, which includes:

- **Tracking both your nutrition and workouts** in a journal or using apps such as My Fitness Pal and the Renpho Scale.
- **Celebrating** the changes you make using your self-care cup gifts.
- **Joining others** on a similar path either online or in person.
- **Continuing the hypnosis, meditation, and other mindset work** you've already begun during your *Wellness Unfu*ked* journey.

Now, let's begin making those small shifts to your diet that result in massive changes!

Remember to keep in mind that nutrition is about more than just eating the right things; it's about eating with mindfulness and intention.

Here's how to start:

- **Mindful Eating**: Make your meals a distraction-free zone. Mindfulness leads to better digestion and satisfaction.
- **Vinegar**: 10 minutes before your first meal of the day, drink 1 tablespoon of apple cider vinegar mixed in a glass of water (with a straw) and enjoy reduced cravings, increased energy, and happy skin.
- **Savory Breakfasts**: Start your day with a protein-rich meal to stabilize your energy levels and mood throughout the day.

To get you started, here are some nutritious breakfast ideas:

- A spinach and feta frittata.
- Toast with hummus, sliced tomato, and a poached egg.
- Oatmeal with raisins, blueberries, local raw honey, and oat milk.
- A smoked tofu wrap with fresh veggies.

And throughout your day, it's important to get in your:

- **Protein (20-35 g/protein/meal during your 6 daily meals)**
  - *Within 30 mins. of your workout & before bed*
  - *Lentils, black beans, peas, soy, tempeh, eggs, chicken breast, tempeh, quinoa, etc.*

- **Complex carbs**
  - *In the morning, as they provide sustained energy*
    - Avoid them at night, as they can be stored as fat.
  - *Oatmeal, brown rice, yams, whole grain bread products, etc.*

- **Simple carbs**
  - *Within 30 mins. of workout*
  - Limit to 25 g (or less) of sugar per day
  - *Juice, sugar, coconut water, etc.*

- **Not-so-fat fats**
  - *Throughout the day*
  - Crucial for muscle-building, joints, hair, and skin
  - *Avocado, nuts, seeds, salmon, flax-seed, fish oil, etc.*

- **Green tea &/or Coffee**
  - *In the morning*

- ▪ *Avoid after 3 p.m., as they can hinder sleep*
  - ○ Green tea boosts metabolism and is loaded with cancer-fighting antioxidants
  - ○ Coffee boosts metabolism and inhibits appetite

- **Fiber**
  - ○ *Throughout the day*
  - ○ To keep you regular, maintain a healthy weight and lower cholesterol
  - ○ *Chia seed, ground flax seed, oats, etc.*

- **Water**
  - ○ *Throughout the day*
  - ○ Drink between .5 and 1 oz./water (34.4 mL/kg and 77.1 mL/kg) for every pound you weigh. For example, if you weigh 150 pounds, you should drink between 75-150 oz. of water daily.
  - ○ To increase energy, maximize weight loss, and improve performance

To track your nutrition and stick to your fitness goals, use apps such as My Fitness Pal. Be sure to add your family, friends, and coaches as friends on this app to create accountability and stay true to your nutrition and hydration goals.

Last but not least, track your progress by embracing the technology that is now available, including things such as the Renpho scale and your smartwatch. The Renpho scale and its alternatives are much more valuable since you can see things like your body water, protein, metabolic age, muscle mass, and visceral fat in real time. This empowers you to see results that may not yet be visible by the traditional scale or even the naked eye.

Detoxing: Unleashing Your Body's Potential

Detoxing isn't just a trend; it's an intensely effective method to improve your fitness, skin health, and mental clarity. It's an essential part of your *Wellness Unfu*ked* journey and helps you reset your system and support your body's natural self-healing abilities. Humans have been engaging in detox practices for millennia, recognizing their benefits for overall health and well-being.

Choosing the Right Detox for You

The key to a successful detox is choosing one that is safe, effective, and aligns with your wellness goals. It's crucial to avoid fad detoxes that promise quick fixes but might actually be detrimental to your health.

To have a lasting impact and enjoy the process, engage in a detox program with friends or community members. This adds an element of fun, accountability, and consistency to the process. Share your journey on social media or within your circle to inspire and motivate each other.

Remember to start simple: If you're new to detoxing, begin with a straightforward approach. A two-week detox focusing on fruits, vegetables, and plenty of water is a great beginning. This simple regimen helps cleanse your system without overwhelming it.

The *Wellness Unfu*ked* Detox Program: For those looking for a more structured plan, try this 9-day, 3-step detox program. It's designed to reduce inflammation, improve digestion, and revitalize your skin:

- **Morning**: Kickstart your day with the juice of half a lemon in a glass of purified water. Use a straw to protect your teeth. After 15 minutes, if you choose, follow up with fresh celery juice.

- **Daytime Diet**: Completely eliminate sugar, flour, and other potential troublemakers like eggs, dairy, gluten, soft drinks, caffeine, and processed foods. These can disrupt your hormonal balance and impede detoxification.
- **Evening**: Wind down with a soothing cup of Chaga, hibiscus, or lemon tea. Before bed, another glass of lemon water helps support overnight detoxification and aids digestion.

When reintroducing foods post-detox, do it gradually. This helps identify any food sensitivities or adverse reactions. Continue incorporating lemon or vinegar water into your daily routine to help manage blood sugar levels, curb cravings, and boost energy.

Integrating these detox strategies into your wellness routine creates a foundation for sustained health and vitality. Detoxing allows you to establish habits that enrich your life and bring you closer to your ultimate health goals.

By the end of your detox, you should be feeling great and getting closer to achieving a vibrant, *Wellness Unfu*ked* lifestyle.

Alcohol & Binging

I decided to get sober after over ten years of heavy drinking because I was tired of blacking out, feeling hungover, and living my life out of control. After my last night of heavy drinking, I felt lost, anxiety-riddled, and stressed about how much money I'd spent and the conversations I didn't remember having. I was also worried about my liver health, as I have alcoholism in my family and know the long-term cost of heavy drinking all too well.

Furthermore, I wanted to reach my full purpose in life. Alcohol was a crutch for me in social situations and was the only way that I let my guard down to be my fullest self. I desired to be my most expressed, authentic self at all times, not just at a Friday night party when I was under the influence and feeling free to dance and just be me.

Although I didn't recognize it at the time, alcohol also sabotaged my own success. This is because when you are under the influence, your subconscious mind is open and receptive to being reprogrammed. For example, if you are intoxicated by alcohol and a friend says, "You're an idiot," you often wake up in the morning and think, "I'm an idiot." This can make it more challenging to change your beliefs, step into a completely new energy, and change your life for the better.

I first got sober by finding a sober friend who kept me accountable and consistently checked in with me. I also placed the affirmation, "I have a good relationship with food and alcohol," into my subconscious using the power of hypnosis, which helped speed up my sobriety journey. Last but not least, I transmuted the energy that I put *toward* alcohol and partying *toward* wellness, movement, and living my definition of success.

Little by little, the pivotal changes empowered me to step into a completely new identity and embrace a sober lifestyle.

Since getting sober in 2021, I've noticed a myriad of health benefits, like clearer skin, more energy, and elevated confidence and focus. Additionally, giving up the bottle has helped my bank account, so I have more funds to do activities I love, buy things that align with who I'm becoming, and invest in myself. Remember that when you decide to drink alcohol regularly, you can end up spending over $10K per year just on drinking alone.

Now, if you desire to drink less in order to speed up your *Wellness Unfu*ked* journey, begin by switching out alcoholic beverages for club soda and other low-sugar alternatives. You can also make a plan that sets out how many drinks you are able to have in a given social situation, let others know about your desire to drink less, or even take a break from alcohol for a set amount of time.

Remember that if you are only attending a social event or spending time with someone because there is alcohol or another substance readily available, it may be helpful to reconsider your relationship with alcohol.

Now, if you are sober-curious and desire to pivot to becoming sober like myself, I recommend connecting with sober communities online or in-person, finding friends and mentors that support your sober journey, and creating consistency and accountability as you step into your new, sober identity. Create new affirmations related to your sobriety journey, and place them into your subconscious using the power of hypnosis.

Exercise for Body and Soul:
Now that you've begun changing how you fuel your body, we're ready to uplevel how you move!

Side effects of exercise for the body and soul include reduced rates of diabetes, improved mood, and deeper sleep. Not to mention, you will notice the weight come off and muscle come on as you exercise your body and soul.

Let's begin by remembering that exercise comes in many forms. Dancing, walking to your car, and using the stairs instead of the elevator all count *toward* your fitness goals.

And remember to pick an exercise plan that helps, rather than hurts, your body.

When I trained without proper form and barely stretched, I began limping after just a few weeks of consistently going to the gym. I soon gave up hope and decided that someone in my physique could not get into shape.

Luckily, great changes happened when I found online and in-person yoga and fitness classes that helped strengthen my joints, tone my muscles, and improve flexibility. I soon realized that for people of my body type, doing yoga regularly was a necessity, as it mimics physical therapy movements.

Over time, I got hooked on fitness when I connected with coaches that I liked and took exercise classes that I loved. This included classes with lots of house and hip-hop music and entertaining coaches who called me out when they knew I wasn't putting in my all during class. This was such a great transition from my past when I would force myself to take yoga classes that just didn't match my vibe.

With this in mind, I invite you to begin the process of enjoying getting fit with people by your side that you like and keep you accountable.

Furthermore, it's about celebrating every step of progress and sticking to a plan that works.

With this in mind, remember that the best fitness routine is the one that you enjoy, can stick with, and matches your current lifestyle (even if you soon plan to make some big changes in your personal or professional life, which I wholeheartedly support!).

With this in mind, I've crafted 3 workout plans for you that maximize toning and weight loss through split-system training, which allows 48 hours of rest between muscle groups.

To keep you accountable and consistent, here's a structured plan to get you started, adaptable to your fitness level:

- **Wellness Unfu*ked Foundation**: Begin with basic strength training and yoga:
    - Monday: Upper body workout / Yoga
    - Tuesday: Lower body & abs / Yoga
    - Wednesday: Active rest
    - Thursday: Upper body workout / Yoga
    - Friday: Lower body workout / Yoga

- **Wellness Unfu*ked Evolution**: Introduce moderate cardio (after six weeks of regular exercise):
    - Monday: Upper body workout / Yoga
    - Tuesday: Lower body & abs / Yoga
    - Wednesday: **Cardio (30+ mins)**
    - Thursday: Upper body workout / Yoga
    - Friday: Lower body workout / Yoga

- **Wellness Unfu*ked Mastery**: Ramp up with high-intensity workouts and sprints (after 12 weeks of regular exercise). This is where you'll maximize muscle, weight loss, and energy gains:
    - Monday: Upper body workout / Yoga
    - Tuesday: Lower body & abs / Yoga
    - Wednesday: **Cardio (30+ mins)**
    - Thursday: Upper body workout / Yoga
    - Friday: Lower body workout / Yoga

- o Saturday: Active rest
- o Sunday: **Cardio & sprints (40+ mins)**

Embrace Your Journey to Wellness Unfu*ked

As you embark on this transformative fitness journey with the *Wellness Unfu*ked* program, remember that personalization is key. Tailor these workout regimens to your body's needs, your schedule, and your personal goals. It's crucial to listen to your body and adjust the routines to fit you perfectly.

After 12 weeks of dedication to your chosen regimen, I highly recommend taking a week of active rest. This will allow your body to recuperate and rebuild stronger than before. It's like taking a short vacation for your muscles, allowing them to recover and grow. Many of my clients have seen significant benefits during this rest period, including losing fat, gaining muscle, and being able to level up their fitness routines even further.

Building a Supportive Fitness Community

Accountability is your secret weapon in achieving and maintaining your fitness goals. Whether you're sweating it out with friends, participating in group classes, or engaging in one-on-one personal training or private yoga sessions, every bit of support counts.

Permanent change is fostered within a community, and investing in your health today will pay dividends in the future. Imagine your future self, perhaps exploring the world in your 80s, vibrant and full of life, all because you made the commitment to your wellness now.

Every Step Counts

And always remember: Done is better than perfect.

Simple activities like walking in the park, swimming, or even choosing a farther parking spot can significantly contribute to your fitness goals. It's these small, consistent actions that build up over time to create lasting change.

Set Your Intentions Now

Today, you stand at the precipice of change. Below, set your intentions and commit to them. Define what level of the *Wellness Unfu*ked* program you are starting with, choose your ideal location for your workouts, and mark the date you will begin this life-enhancing journey.

Try This: Create Your Implementation Intention.

- **Decide which exercise routine level is best for you now:** [Wellness Unfu*ked Foundation, Elevation, or Mastery]
- **Location:** Specify where you will be exercising
- **Start Date:** Set a specific start date for your routine

By documenting your plan, you make a tangible commitment to your wellness journey. Begin today, and let every day be a step toward the change you wish to see in your life, your body, and ultimately, the world. Let's move forward together, creating a life filled with health, joy, and unshakable wellness.

Lifestyle Adjustments for Transformational Wellness

Embarking on a wellness journey isn't just about adjusting your diet and exercise routine; it's about transforming your entire lifestyle to support your long-term health and happiness. Reflecting deeply on the lifestyle changes necessary to elevate your fitness journey is crucial for making the experience enjoyable and sustainable.

For myself, transformative changes included a complete career shift, relocating to a new city, and eliminating alcohol from my life. Despite consuming a diet rich in organic produce, healthy proteins, and fats, the adverse effects of alcohol consumption and processed foods were undeniable. After cutting out alcohol, I experienced a massive increase in energy, a significant clearing of my acne, and a surge in positive thinking. Similarly, embracing a career in wellness and changing my environment catalyzed my fitness goals to new heights.

Many of my clients have also found success by making substantial lifestyle adjustments. For some, this meant setting what I like to call "love boundaries" with toxic people, cutting out sugar and flour entirely during their weight loss journey, or integrating joyful activities like dance into their weekly routine. For others, more drastic changes were necessary, such as changing careers, ending long-term relationships, or moving to a new environment to better support their wellness goals.

Now, it's Your Turn!

It's time for you to explore the potential blind spots in your lifestyle that could be holding you back from reaching your ultimate fitness and wellness goals. Engage in a free-writing session to identify lifestyle, mindset, and nutrition/fitness hacks that could catapult you to the next level and facilitate lasting change.

Lifestyle Brain Dump Exercise (10 minutes):

- Set a timer for ten minutes.

- Write freely about any aspect of your lifestyle that feels misaligned with your wellness goals.
- Consider changes in your environment, relationships, career, and daily habits.
- Don't edit or censor your thoughts; let the ideas flow to uncover insights that might be hiding just beneath the surface.

This exercise is designed to uncover deep insights and empower you to make informed decisions that align with a holistic approach to wellness. By identifying and implementing strategic lifestyle adjustments, you position yourself on a path not just to meet your fitness goals but to exceed them and thrive in all areas of your life.

Remember, every change you implement is a stepping stone *toward* a healthier, happier you.

CHAPTER 9

REST AND RECHARGE - MASTERING SLEEP AND STRESS MANAGEMENT

Prioritizing quality sleep and effective stress management isn't just about feeling better—it's about fundamentally enhancing your life.

When I battled insomnia and anxiety, I could barely function in both my work and personal life. I struggled with low energy, skin problems, and strained relationships.

Without the energy needed for everyday activities like cooking, exercising, and meditating, maintaining wellness seemed impossible. However, by establishing routines to soothe my nervous system and manage stress, I achieved the best sleep of my life—and you can too.

The Transformative Power of Sleep:

Sleep is the cornerstone of physical and mental health. It boosts productivity and is critical in your fitness journey. Muscle growth and weight loss kick into gear during deep, restorative sleep. When you get in eight or more quality hours of sleep, reduced cortisol levels signal to your body that it is safe to repair and rejuvenate.

Strategies for Optimal Sleep:

Achieving high-quality sleep requires more than just going to bed early; it involves managing your energy and time effectively. External stressors like demanding jobs or too much screen time before bed can disrupt your sleep patterns.

Personally, I began getting the best sleep of my life when I began ending every day exhausted from exercise, movement, and activities that made my heart sing. My sleep also improved upon integrating hypnosis into my evening routine and changing my environment to ensure optimal sleep.

Now, let's begin! Here's how to create an environment conducive to good sleep:

1. **Assess Your Lifestyle**: Take an honest look at what fills your life with energy and what drains it. Are stressful work conditions or toxic relationships causing you anxiety that keeps you up at night? Sometimes, the solution is as significant as changing jobs or setting firm boundaries with people who deplete your energy.
2. **Create the Right Environment**: Improve your sleep quality by ensuring complete darkness and quiet in your bedroom. Blackout curtains, eye masks, and earplugs can dramatically improve your sleep environment.
3. **Incorporate Supplements**: Certain supplements like magnesium and CBD can promote relaxation and improve sleep quality without the side effects of prescription sleep aids.
4. **Embrace Pre-Sleep Rituals**: Engage in calming activities such as breathwork, meditation, or hypnosis before bed. These practices help settle your mind and prepare your body for sleep. I recommend exploring the guided sessions that you can find on the Wellness Unfu*ked Course Website and my YouTube channel, which are specifically designed for relaxation and stress relief.

Reflective Practice for Sleep Improvement:

Below, you'll find space to jot down the aspects of your life that impact your sleep. Reflect on the changes you can make to enhance your sleep quality and overall well-being.

My Sleep Improvement Plan:

- Issues Impacting Sleep:
- Possible Solutions:
- Action Steps:

By understanding and implementing these strategies, you transform sleep from a mere necessity to a powerful ally in your wellness journey. Remember, good sleep and stress management aren't just about avoiding fatigue; they're about setting the foundation for a vibrant, energized life. Equip yourself with these tools and watch as every aspect of your health improves along with your sleep.

SECTION 4:

IGNITE YOUR MIND - THE MENTAL PILLAR

MASTER YOUR MINDSET – REWRITING LIMITING BELIEFS

Welcome to a transformative chapter in your journey with "Wellness Unfu*ked" where we dig even more deeply into the very foundations of what makes you, you. It's time to confront and flip those limiting beliefs that have stealthily shaped your reality and constrained your potential.

Limiting beliefs, those persistent and often misleading scripts, typically embed themselves amid our childhood and adolescent years. Rooted in misinterpretations of experiences or inherited from societal, familial, or cultural narratives, these beliefs solidify within your subconscious mind, which drives 90% of your mental functioning.

Yet, here's the empowering truth: your personality isn't permanent, and your future is not fixed.

You hold the power to recalibrate your mind and, by extension, transform your life and body. If you find yourself battling with issues like weight challenges, chronic skin conditions, or an overall sense of fatigue, it might not just be physical. These could be manifestations of a deeper mental narrative that desperately needs rewriting.

In this chapter, I'm your partner in peeling back the layers of outdated beliefs to reveal the vibrant wellness warrior that dwells within you now. We'll identify these saboteurs and transform them into affirmations that don't just whisper but shout from the rooftops: "Yes, I can!"

Those who have achieved lasting change—whether it's maintaining sobriety, achieving long-term weight loss, or simply finding peace—haven't merely altered their habits; they've revolutionized their entire belief systems.

Think of this process as a wardrobe change for your soul, where we swap out the old, ill-fitting thoughts for new, tailored affirmations that fit who you truly are and who you are destined to become. Let's embark on this mind makeover and dress your soul in nothing but the best!

Step 1: Identify and Challenge Limiting Beliefs

Let's start with a quick, powerful meditation—just six minutes. Ask yourself these probing questions:

- What do I believe about my physical form?
- How worthy do I feel of achieving my desires?
- Why might I believe I'm not worthy?

Now, jot down whatever pops up. These could be things like, "I'm not fit enough," "I'm not attractive," or "I don't have time to get healthy."

Step 2: Flip It and Reverse It!

Now, let's take those limiting beliefs and turn them completely around. This step is about transforming each of those restrictive thoughts into powerful, positive affirmations that resonate with who you are and who you aim to be. Begin each affirmation with a potent "I am," "I have," or another statement that begins with "I...," and let it be a mantra that you not only believe in but one that redefines your reality, such as:

- I am fit, strong, and healthy.
- I am beautiful.
- I have a good relationship with food and alcohol.

Once you've constructed these empowering statements, write them down and place them where they will be an unavoidable part of your daily routine. Place them on your home mirror or another visible location that consistently reminds you of your potential, worth, and who you are becoming.

But let's take it a step further. After adding these affirmations to your *Unfu*ked Affirmations* Worksheet in the appendices, record these latest affirmations on your device and make them the soundtrack of your morning routine. As you dress, eat, or commute, let these affirmations fill your ears and heart, reinforcing their power and your belief in them.

Next, integrate these affirmations into your subconscious. Utilize my specially designed *Unfu*ked Hypnosis Recording*, which is available on the Wellness Unfu*ked Course website at <u>wellness.fitergy.co</u>.

In a relaxed, hypnotic state, not only repeat these affirmations but truly feel each one. Visualize the script of your desired life playing out as if it were real. Continue to engage in this hypnosis daily to lay down the foundations of your new belief system. Over time, watch as your life transforms—aligning your body, mind, and spirit with your new beliefs, new energy, new you!

Through this intentional practice of affirmation and visualization, you are not just hoping for change; you are actively installing a new framework in your mind that will manifest in your external world.

Let's reprogram those old tapes and step into a vibrant, unfu*ked wellness that truly reflects your inner strength and beauty.

Step 3: Cultivating a Growth Mindset

It's all about loving the process, not just the end game. Celebrate every little victory along the way, not just the big milestones. If you nailed a healthy breakfast, give yourself a high-five. If you chose a walk over a TV binge, do a little victory dance.

Here's how to keep that mindset sparkling:

- Every day, write down one small win.
- Reward yourself with something sweet (like a moment to yourself, a favorite tea, or a relaxing bath) that reinforces the new fabulous you.

As you reinforce positive behavior and take power away from your inner critic, get ready for a life, body, and mind that you love!

Your body is in your mind. When you feel and think in alignment with the person you are becoming, it is only a matter of time until you experience profound changes in your physical form and life, whether it be your energy, weight, or even who you're dating.

Furthermore, your personality is not permanent. Even now, as an adult, you get to decide what parts of you to develop and enhance and what aspects of yourself to leave in a past season of your life.

Cognitive Restructuring Exercises

Great changes happened in my body, mind, and life when I stopped taking myself too seriously. I used to shame rather than embrace my humanity. I had unrealistic expectations about how I looked, what I did, and who I was.

Little by little, I shifted my perspective on my perceived failures. This started with small things like laughing upon falling over during the inversions section of a yoga class and blossomed into me feeling blessed, rather than devastated, upon being unfollowed by someone online.

And since loving those parts of me that are imperfect, embracing both the highs and the lows, and creating a new identity, I've attracted even greater happiness, love, health, and success.

And remember: falling down is a part of the process of your *Wellness Unfu*ked* journey. In fact, falling down is when we learn and grow, and it also builds valuable skills like empathy, wisdom, and a deeper understanding of others.

Having a positive mindset is also one of the greatest keys to long-term success. And although negativity can get you started on your *Wellness Unfu*ked* journey, it simply cannot keep you going when times get tough. Rather, people who make sustained changes in their bodies, minds, and lives do so with positivity and the energy of love.

And so, with good reason, remember to treat yourself kindly as you make wonderful pivots in your personal and professional life.

With this in mind, it's paramount to focus on what you gained during those darker times. Additionally, continue those activities that keep you unconsciously positive, regardless of the three-dimensional results of your hard work.

Beginning today, start speaking to yourself as though you are your own best friend!

Now, if you are still facing issues related to self-kindness during your *Wellness Unfu*ked* journey, it may be time to have a conversation with the many beings that make up you. This technique empowers you to shift identities in order to create long-term, sustainable change.

Most people have around 6-8 people in their consciousness and subconscious minds that "run the game" and dictate their emotions, beliefs, actions, and lives.

Begin by naming the beings within you, and setting aside just ten minutes for everyone to have a conversation with yourself.

Together, create a plan where you give control to the being in you that supports your desired body, mind, and life.

For me, amazing changes happened when I decided to give complete control to the personality that I created in my mind, which I named "Luke Yoga." This person is confident, dedicated, humorous, and self-compassionate as I continue to expand in abundance, success, health, and love.

Meanwhile, I decided to take power away from those personalities that used to cause me to self-sabotage, including such beings as "Luke the Partier," "Luke the Worrier," and "Hardass Luke." Some of these personalities were placed in the basement, some were put outside to find a new home, and one personality type was even executed. These crucial steps empowered me to get and stay sober, launch my wellness business, and even call in true love.

Sometimes, the beings that used to make up my inner essence still visit the home that is my mind. However, the difference is that they now only visit for a short while and do not have control over the wiring of my conscious and subconscious mind.

When these uninvited guests pay me a visit, I treat them well and release them through techniques such as breathwork, yoga, fitness, and hypnosis.

Now, let's begin! List the beings that make up you, have a conversation with them to find clarity and direction, and take actions that embrace the identity that aligns with who you are becoming.

Try This: Have a Conversation with Your Inner Beings.

Name the inner beings that make up you:

1.
2.
3.
4.
5.
6.
7.
8.

After having a conversation with your inner beings, respond to the following questions::
- Who is *now* in control?
- Who *lost* control?
- What were your greatest takeaways?
- What will you do to cope when and if former beings that used to have control visit your mind?

CHAPTER 11

MINDFULNESS AND MEDITATION - INNER PEACE AND CLARITY

We're living in a time of ultimate distraction, where our attention is pulled in countless directions. That's why mindfulness and meditation aren't just nice-to-haves; they're must-haves. These practices cut through the noise, helping you focus, reduce stress, and get those creative juices flowing.

Before embracing mindfulness, I struggled with my sleep, health, and direction in life. Only after creating a mindfulness routine that works for my busy schedule have I been able to manifest my desires rather than fall victim to my circumstances and life's many distractions.

I began with small things, like taking a few deep breaths upon waking, and now regularly meditate in the morning and listen to hypnosis before going to bed.

Long meditations are especially helpful when making big decisions. This is because when you are in theta waves during meditation, you connect with the collective consciousness and are no longer ego-driven. During deep meditations, you can access the ideas of everyone in the universe rather than your own limited prefrontal cortex, which only makes up 5% of your mind. You are able to access the rest of your brain and get into gamma and theta waves, where true magic happens.

The most creative ideas come to you with ease and clarity when you are in flow. Flow is a positive mental state where you are fully immersed in an activity and are able to get sh*t done effortlessly and easily.

And luckily, achieving flow becomes easier when you practice mindfulness on the regular. That's because mindfulness helps you filter out distractions and focus on what matters.

Your meditation routine will amplify the similarly positive benefits offered through your workouts, yoga class, and/or breathwork session, which also help you get into a flow state.

Get ready for some massive changes in your life! Soon, you'll notice epiphanies hit you like never before. You'll notice opportunities here at this very moment.

And you'll begin living in present-moment awareness, where transformation takes place.

Let's begin!

Embrace Mindfulness
Start with just 5 minutes of meditation each day. Begin your meditation immediately after waking up and using the bathroom. Set your alarm just 5 minutes before your normal time to rise so that you're not rushed to complete your regular meditation routine.

Use an app like Insight Timer, which has wonderful background music, or just sit in silence. Write down any insights or feelings that arise. Over time, increase your meditation time to fit your lifestyle and goals.

If you are struggling to meditate to background music or silence alone, begin with guided meditations. Download Presence: Meditate & Thrive, Insight Timer, or another alternative app to your device, and begin one of their guided meditation programs that match your *Wellness Unfu*ked* goals."

Some wonderful meditation series to begin your mindfulness journey include the following:

- 21 Days of Abundance Meditation Series (Presence: Meditate & Thrive App & Spotify)
- Miraculous Relationships Meditation Series (Presence: Meditate & Thrive App)
- 7 Days to Relieve Stress & Anxiety Program (Presence: Meditate & Thrive App)

Information Overload & Living Mindfully

Although it's so wonderful that we can use our devices to connect with anyone, anywhere, we are now consuming more information than ever before.

Scientists have found that the average person today processes as much as 74 GB of information per day through their device. This number increases by about 5% every year. And just five hundred years ago, the average person consumed this same amount of information in their entire lifetime!

On top of this, when we look things up online or even walk around the neighborhood, we are now distracted by ads, notifications, news, and pervasive background noise, which can overload our brains, distract us from our goals, and cause us to feel drained, stressed, and overwhelmed.

As such, it's now more important than ever to set boundaries with technology and social media.

If you are currently experiencing a heightened sense of burnout related to your gadgets and devices, begin sometime this month with a 24-hour technology or social media detox. If you're an active user of your device, let your friends, family, and followers know in advance so they are not worried when you don't immediately respond to their DMs and comments.

Remember that in the long term, technology detoxes are so worth it. They will likely open up further creativity, joy, health, and happiness.

And on a daily basis, remember that technology is a tool, not a tether. And so, let's now set some routine boundaries with your gadgets! Begin with:

- No phones during the first hour of your morning and the last hour before bed.
- During your tech-free hour, do something that enriches your soul—read, journal, meditate, or just be.

If you wake up at 6 a.m., you should only begin using your phone at 7 a.m. It's best to only check your device after meditating, listening to your *Wellness Unfu*ked* script recordings, getting ready, and eating a healthy, hearty, savory breakfast.

And if you go to sleep at 10 p.m., make it a rule to no longer use your devices after 9 p.m., as this allows your mind to relax and "power down." This simple step ensures that you get amazing, deep sleep and wake up recharged in the morning.

Furthermore, if you have activities that require your undivided attention, do not check social media or other forms of technology before completing the task at hand.

Even while writing this book at this very moment, I have not checked my social media today, as I desire to get into a flow state and make this book beyond amazing for you and countless other *Wellness Unfu*ked* readers!

For a more structured approach to both your evening and morning routine, refer to the Unfu*ked Morning and Evening Rituals in the appendices of this book, which will ensure that you are taking all of the steps necessary. Little by little, you'll notice massive changes in your body, mind, and life as you prioritize mindful living.

Also, don't forget to check in with yourself throughout the day. A deep breath or a quick walk can recharge your batteries and keep you centered, regardless of what comes your way.

As you continue to embrace mindful living, get ready to regularly wake up on the right side of the bed, excited and ready for your day!

EMOTIONAL INTELLIGENCE - NAVIGATING YOUR INNER WORLD

Our emotions are visitors—some pleasant, some challenging. They all come with messages, teaching us about our deepest selves. But not every emotional response serves us in the long run.

Furthermore, emotions need to be experienced and addressed in order to go up the tone scale and experience higher levels of awareness.

In my own journey, I used to push down and suppress my emotions when I was depressed and hopeless. At the time, I didn't know that lower feelings on the tone scale, like covert hostility, anger, and even boredom, typically need to be experienced in order for you to feel content, joyful, and blissful.

Only after getting comfortable experiencing and going through my emotions have I been able to access higher states of awareness and ultimately change my vibration.

Your vibration is the feeling people get when you walk into a room. Other words for this are your aura or your energy.

And when you change your vibration, you change your life!

Since like energy attracts like, more high-vibe people, experiences, and things are magnetized *toward* you when you raise your vibration. Get ready for relationships, health, and success at a whole new level.

Now, let's begin navigating your inner world in order to accelerate your *Wellness Unfu*ked* journey.

Managing Emotions

When emotions run high, it's easy to revert to old coping mechanisms like stress eating, binge drinking, or zoning out. I've been there and used to be addicted to the pain and pleasure of maladaptive coping mechanisms. This led me down a path of pity, shame, and depression and even exacerbated my addictions to alcohol, weed, and scrolling on social media.

Luckily, amazing changes happened when I began managing my emotions rather than reacting to them.

When you experience challenging emotions, begin by taking a few deep breaths. Next, take actions that help you healthily deal with your feelings. This may mean a walk, getting into nature, taking a yoga class, or calling a friend.

And remember: You are not your emotions.

Your emotions are like guests who are only with you for a limited amount of time. Sometimes, these emotions are so dark and intense that they take all of the furniture, belongings, and cherished items of your inner world. Although this is often challenging at the time, remember that such emotions are simultaneously clearing this space for your inner growth, expansion, and ascension.

In fact, experiencing "negative" emotions is a good sign, as you must experience these feelings in order to later experience higher, more desirable emotions.

However, if you are feeling an emotion for an extended period of time, and it doesn't seem to be leaving:

- Acknowledge and name the emotion.
- Feel where this emotion is in your body.
- Decide what emotion you desire to replace this emotion with.
- Breathe in as you notice this emotion, and exhale to release and replace this undesired feeling.

And always remember to ask yourself what you need at this moment. You can always do one of the activities that you know fills your cup when times get hard.

And often, you'll need to force yourself to do this self-loving activity, *even when you don't feel like doing it.*

Know that you are not alone in managing your emotions, and help is out there. This help may come in the form of reaching out to a friend or tapping into traditional therapy, energy medicine like reiki, or even movement like a fitness class.

Regardless, if you now feel hopeless, or you or someone that you know is considering ending his, her, or their life, you can call 988, the suicide and crisis lifeline in the USA.

Tools for Self-Regulation and Empathy

Understanding what triggers your emotions is key. Is it a specific person, a type of event, or maybe an old memory? Here's how to handle these triggers:

- Change your environment to reduce negative triggers.
- Reframe how you view these triggers—every challenge has a silver lining.

And remember, regular check-ins with yourself are crucial. What does each part of you need to thrive? How can they work together to support your emotional well-being?

Use the space below to free write about your action plan. How will you manage your emotions better? What steps will you take today to embrace a healthier, more emotionally intelligent life?

By mastering your mindset, embracing mindfulness, and navigating your emotional world with intelligence and empathy, you're setting yourself up for success in every area of your life. This is how you ignite your mind and set your entire life ablaze with possibility!

SECTION 5:

TRANSFORM YOUR LIFE - THE LIFE PILLAR

CHAPTER 13

WELLNESS IN ACTION - HABITS, ROUTINES, AND RITUALS

Welcome to the best years of your life!

As we venture into this exciting part of our *Wellness Unfu*ked* journey, let's roll up our sleeves and develop some life-transforming habits, routines, and daily rituals that both nourish your soul and get you vibing higher every single day. In this section, it's all about making those small yet mighty changes that turn into big victories in your wellness quest!

Oftentimes, the smallest and most consistent habits, routines, and rituals have the greatest impact on your long-term goals, beliefs, and desires. I only overcome internalized homophobia, for example, by consistently listening to my self-loving affirmations, saying them to myself, and doing hypnosis, fitness, and yoga *every single day* with people who lift me higher.

Nonetheless, I still continue to offer myself grace on my own routine when I'm traveling, just returned from one of my favorite music concerts (yes, I love Coachella!), or am in a transitional period in my life (like a new love, new home, or new career). So remember to practice self-compassion as you make these subtle and profound changes to your daily rituals.

Keep in mind that there is not a one-size-fits-all approach when creating your daily morning and evening routine. That's why I offer you a baseline example of what's worked for me, my clients, and others out there on similar *Wellness Unfu*ked* journeys. And that's also why it's critical to continuously alter your routine during the ensuing weeks, months, and years in order to optimize progress *toward* your ever-changing goals.

Creating Your Personal Rituals

It's showtime! Let's set up daily rituals that are perfectly structured to fit your life! Remember, what works for a high-flying executive might not jive with a creative soul who is stirring up the art world. The key is customization—finding what resonates with your lifestyle and goals.

Start your day with intention and end it with gratitude. Here's a sneak peek into a day in the life of a lifestyle coach aiming for the stars in business, love, and health:

Example Morning Routine:

- 6:10 AM: Rise and shine!
- 6:10 – 6:30 AM: Meditate and journal your way into the day.
- 6:30 – 7:00 AM: Prep for the day while listening to your unfu*ked affirmations, visualization script, and letter from your 120-year-old self.
- 7:00 – 8:00 AM: Energize with a yoga session or workout.
- 8:00 – 9:00 AM: Nourishing breakfast and tidy-up time.
- 9:00 – 9:30 AM: Gear up with a quick digital check-in before diving into work.

Example Evening Routine:

- 9:00 PM: Disconnect from digital distractions.
- 9:00 – 9:30 PM: Wind down, prep for tomorrow, and reflect with some light journaling or reading.

- 9:30 – 10:00 PM: Drift into dreamland with a soothing hypnosis session.
- 10:00 PM: Lights out for a rejuvenating sleep.

To keep you accountable, refer to the Unfu*ked Morning & Evening Rituals checklists in the appendices of this book. Remember to personalize your ritual to match your schedule and adjust as needed when traveling and experiencing other fluctuations to your normal routine.

If you are currently unable to squeeze in all of the above steps during this season of your life, begin with grace and add just one new activity into your morning and evening routine every week.

Now, if it's simply impossible to do all of the above steps during this time of your life (yes, I know what it's like to have 16-hour workdays during medical school!), celebrate those self-loving steps that you can take to start and end your day right. Sometimes, turning your phone on Do Not Disturb and meditating for 6 minutes before going to sleep is an amazing end to a hectic day.

Remember to also add your own flavor to the above morning ritual, including such optional additions as prayer, breathwork, or simply lighting a candle with amazing scents before beginning your workday.

You know what raises your vibe, so let's start doing that now every single day!

Tracking Progress and Staying Accountable

Make your routine dynamic—adjust as you evolve, and don't sweat it if life throws a curveball. Even if you miss a day, remember to treat yourself with kindness and jump back in.

Above all else, consistency beats perfection!

Stay motivated by rewarding yourself for each small success. Maybe it's a peaceful walk, a spa day, or just some quiet time with your favorite book. Keep a record of your daily wins and share your journey with someone who cheers you on, whether it's through our vibrant Facebook community or a close buddy who's also on their *Wellness Unfu*ked* journey.

Use the *Wellness Unfu*ked* Morning and Evening Ritual Checklist and the space below to create your personalized morning and evening rituals. Announce this new plan to your family, mentors, coaches, and those who are cheering you on during your *Wellness Unfu*ked* journey so that they know to honor these amazing changes you are making and support you on your path.

CHAPTER 14

RELATIONSHIPS AND CONNECTION - FUELING YOUR WELL-BEING

Remember that the richness of your life is measured by the richness of your relationships. When you surround yourself with folks who lift you up, you're not just living—you're thriving!

Personally, I've experienced bountiful love, health, and happiness only since connecting with friends, partners, and even clients who align with me at my core. Simultaneously, magnificent changes have happened since distancing myself from people who aren't energetically aligned.

Nurturing Healthy Relationships and Setting Boundaries

It's crucial to cultivate relationships that nourish your soul. Sometimes, that means setting firm boundaries, even with those we love. Love boundaries help you cherish these relationships without compromising your peace.

If a relationship feels more draining than fulfilling, it may be time to reassess. For those relationships that can't be mended, gracefully letting go might be the key to preserving your well-being.

Nurturing Healthy Relationships and Setting Boundaries

Healthy relationships should energize you, not deplete you. If you feel uplifted, supported, and valued, you're on the right track. However, if interactions leave you feeling drained or less than yourself, it might be time to rethink these connections.

Quick Guide to Recognizing Unhealthy Relationships:

- **Drama and Negativity**: They consistently bring a cloud of negativity.
- **Lack of Support**: They show little to no interest or joy in your accomplishments.
- **Energy-Draining Interactions**: Conversations leave you more exhausted than energized.

If these signs are familiar, it is critical that you consider setting boundaries or possibly stepping back from these relationships. However, some relationships exhibit deeper issues, often related to narcissistic traits, which can be even more damaging.

Traits of Narcissistic Individuals:

- **Vague and General**: They often speak in broad generalities.
- **Pessimistic**: They predominantly share or exaggerate bad news.
- **Distorted Communication**: They tend to alter or worsen information.
- **Unresponsive to Change**: They do not improve from therapy or coaching.
- **Troublemakers**: They frequently create problems for others.
- **Misplaced Blame**: They habitually blame others inaccurately for their problems.
- **Unfinished Projects**: They start many tasks but rarely complete them.
- **Lack of Remorse**: They show no regret or shame for their actions.

- **Destructive Alignment**: They support groups or activities that are harmful.
- **Property Misunderstanding**: They often do not respect ownership or personal boundaries.

Recognizing these traits can be the first step in handling challenging interactions. Setting "love boundaries" is essential—limiting contact to manageable amounts, choosing less personal communication methods like text or email, or in severe cases, cutting ties completely. Sometimes, creating distance is required to preserve your mental health and well-being.

Connect in Joyful Spaces

As you attract positive relationships and distance yourself from more challenging connections, immerse yourself in environments that resonate with your spirit, whether it's a Zumba class, an art workshop, or vibrant online communities. These spaces not only provide relaxation but also attract individuals who share your values and passions.

Live Authentically and Embrace New Experiences

Authentic living attracts authentic relationships. Embrace activities that reflect your true self, and give yourself permission to explore new experiences—whether it's traveling, joining a retreat, or attending a cultural event. These experiences open doors for you to meet like-minded individuals and expand your social circle in meaningful ways.

Recognize and Foster Positive Relationships

Positive relationships are key to enhancing your life quality, accelerating your personal growth, and healing past wounds. Here are indicators of positive, uplifting connections:

- **Clear and Positive Communication**: They share good news eagerly and handle bad news with care, maintaining clarity and positivity in their communications.
- **Effective Growth**: They respond positively to coaching and therapy, demonstrating a commitment to personal development.
- **Reliability and Integrity**: They complete what they start and hold themselves accountable for their actions.
- **Supportive Nature**: They engage in constructive actions and support groups that aim for betterment, actively resisting harmful behaviors.
- **Respect for Others**: They show genuine respect for property and personal boundaries, advocating for fairness and respect in all interactions.

When your friends, partners, and even business contacts exhibit the above indicators, you're set up for success, happiness, and love. This is in stark contrast to those unhealthy relationships that often cause us to "rollercoaster" mentally, physically, and spiritually.

Now that we've explored the features of both types of relationships, it's time to decide which people to align yourself with and which to set some firm boundaries.

What steps will you be taking to foster and build your dream soul tribe?

Finding and Keeping Your Soulmate

Finding a soulmate can profoundly enrich your life, not just romantically but in all aspects, enhancing your happiness, health, and even financial well-being. Remember, the world is vast, and there are many potential soulmates out there. Embrace the abundance of opportunities available in today's connected world—whether online or in person—and remember to present your authentic self.

Creating Genuine Connections

1. **Be True and Vulnerable**: Authenticity attracts the right people. Be honest about who you are; this authenticity will draw people who truly resonate with you.
2. **Align with Core Values**: Ensure potential soulmates share your core values and life goals. Compatibility in these areas is often more important than physical or material attributes. If your partner does not share your core values, which affect most of your important decisions, one partner or both partners will begin to resent one another sooner or later. For example, if one partner is a highly devout Christian and your partner is an atheist, this could create significant friction when planning your marriage or raising your children. Self-awareness is key! So, let's begin by exploring your core values. Some examples of core values include achievement, adventure, career, children, diversity, empathy, family, god, wealth, spirituality, stability, and travel. Now, let's reflect:
   a. What are your top 5 core values?
   b. What are your long-term goals in the relationship (marriage, kids, pets, etc.)?
3. **Journal Your Desires**: Clearly define the qualities you seek in a partner. This clarity will help you recognize the right person when they come along.

Keep in mind that although it's important to decide what type of partner you desire, it's similarly important to be flexible and that you may meet your dream partner who has qualities that you could never have wished for and may lack some of those qualities you would have loved. For example, one soulmate that I dated, who was a fabulous match, lacked empathy but had telepathy. His psychic abilities turned out to be so quite exhilarating and helpful in my life and our partnership.

Embrace Independence and Detach with Flair

Now that you've taken steps to explore your core values and decided on the characteristics of your dream partner, let's kickstart your fabulous journey of self-love!

Even if you're now calling in your soulmate, it's simultaneously time to redefine what it means to be single and thriving.

Whether you're flying solo or seeking your soulmate, remember: you attract people at the same frequency, so let's ensure that you're doing you to your fullest!

Embrace Your Fabulous Solo Life

Rock your single status like a boss! Starting today, cultivate a lifestyle bursting with joy, passions, and fulfillment—partner or not. This isn't just about being okay on your own; it's about being spectacularly unstoppable.

A full, vibrant life makes you irresistibly attractive to others who are just as complete.

Now, if you're still feeling frustrated because of the longer-than-expected timeline of attracting a soulmate, let's still feel good now. Do what lights you up even before your soulmate shows up.

If you're still feeling lost, write down on a piece of paper what feelings you desire in response to being in a relationship with your dream partner.

Now, go ahead and journal what activities you can do to activate those feelings! The possibilities are endless. Examples include a self-love trip, getting fit and healthy, or finally beginning that dream business you've always been thinking of launching.

And as you uplevel your vibe through doing things that light you up now, get ready to magnetize your dream partner at a whole new level, as like attracts like.

Keep your eyes peeled for your future boo in the present moment, as you may find your soulmate in unexpected places like your friend's FB/IG Stories, while taking a walk down the street, or on the train.

Nowadays, 90% of new relationships begin online, so remember to spruce up your online presence to show all of your amazing, beautiful, and unique attributes.

This way, people will be attracted to what makes you, you!

And remember that you attract your soulmate while on your soul path.

And all of the steps you're taking are only adding value to the fabulous, wonderful soul that is you!

Relationship Dynamics: Do You, Boo!

Every relationship should boost you higher, not bring you down. Focus on nurturing connections that inspire, uplift, and challenge you to grow. And the most crucial relationship? The one with yourself—treat it like the ultimate love story.

How are you showing yourself love now?

Setting the Stage for Soulful Connections

Before diving into the dating pool, ensure you're clear about who you are and what you're looking for. Sprinkle your dating profiles with honesty about your core values and share what makes your heart sing—whether it's your love for dance-offs, your cooking skills, or your nerdy love for books. Declare your intentions to the universe, and watch as it conspires to help you find matches that are really worth the swipe.

Longevity in Love: More Than Just Good Looks

Remember, the strongest relationships are built on shared dreams, belly laughs, and mutual respect—not just on looks or bank accounts. Treat every date as a step in learning more about what truly makes relationships stick.

Dating as Discovery

Think of dating as an adventure where each experience teaches you more about love and yourself. Keep an open mind—sometimes, the most unexpected people teach us the most important lessons.

For My Fabulous Queer Family

Being queer is your superpower, and sharing your identity is your choice. Whether you flaunt your rainbow or enjoy a more private journey, know that every shade of you is perfect.

Personally, I choose to share my sexuality on my dating profile in order to filter those that may not love my queer essence. This has also aided me in loving myself more wholeheartedly and attracted people of all genders who appreciate this side of me.

Nonetheless, sharing personal things like your sexual preferences and other attributes like your racial background, political beliefs, and even your zodiac sign on public spaces like dating apps are all personal preferences.

Being transparent either now or later is a personal decision.

Above all else, it's important to ask yourself what feels good to you when creating your public dating profile.

Conscious Uncoupling

Not every connection is meant to last, and that's okay! If someone steps back from your fabulous self, send them off with a blessing. Remember, their exit is not a rejection—it's redirection to something better. Take the lessons, cherish the good times, and when you're ready, return to the dating scene with even more direction, wisdom, and authenticity.

If someone that you fell for didn't work out, it's important to give yourself the space to heal in order to return to the dating world even stronger.

After a relationship ends, consider:

- What did I learn from this relationship?
- How can I practice grace *toward* myself during this transition?
- Why were we not a good match?

Remember that if you are still in love with someone you recently uncoupled with, it's critical to give yourself at least three months of no contact. You can let your former partner know this so that they can respect your boundaries.

Take proactive actions to get over your ex, like unfollowing/muting them on social media, changing their name to YDB (You Deserve Better) on your phone, and even letting your friends and family know that you prefer to no longer discuss them.

These steps give you time and space to heal, strengthen your relationship with yourself, and return stronger to the dating world.

And for those of you who desire complete spiritual separation from your previous partner, remember that there are energy practices that can help you step into a new, independent identity. I even offer my clients tools like a Getting Over Your Ex Hypnosis and Cord Cutting Ceremony.

If any of this sounds interesting, contact me, and I'll send you more information. I got you!

This Week's Love Mission

Get proactive about pulling in that dreamboat or building a stronger bond with your current flame. Here are some powerful steps to amp up your love life:

- **Self-Love Luxuries**: Spoil yourself rotten. Date yourself as you would someone you adore.
- **Profile Perfection**: Jazz up your online dating profiles. Be bold, be bright, be you.
- **Social Butterfly**: Flap those wings! Attend social events or try new activities where you can meet new faces or maybe bump into "The One."
- **Tell the World**: Let your friends know you're ready to meet someone special. Sometimes, they can be your best matchmakers.

So, what's your move going to be? Let's make this week one for the love books!

CHAPTER 15

PURPOSE AND FULFILLMENT - ALIGNING WITH YOUR TRUE CALLING

If you want to shrink your life's problems, grow your purpose! Trust me, when you live in alignment with your true calling, life doesn't just improve; it sings. Those who align with their purpose are known to lead healthier, happier lives—they're less prone to illness, enjoy longer lifespans, and bounce back quicker during tough times.

But finding that purpose? Now, that's a journey not everyone finds easy.

Some people know their calling from childhood, while others, especially those blessed with a spectrum of talents or those who've had to hustle just to survive, might find it more complex. But here's the real tea: if you don't get in touch with your purpose, all the success, money, or perfect health won't mean a thing. You've got to dig deep—because living without real purpose is like grasping at happiness with a hole in your hand.

My Own Twisty Path to Purpose

My path wasn't straight out of a fairy tale. I spent years making choices based on what others thought best and ignored my inner voice. I was all set to be a doctor—can you imagine? Me, in a lab coat, unhappy and unfulfilled because I was chasing someone else's dream. It nearly broke me.

But when I finally started asking myself the right questions, everything changed. I began my *Wellness Unfu*ked* path and never looked back.

So, let's get personal. Think about it:

- **What's the best decision you ever made?** How did you come to it—was it a gut feeling, or did someone nudge you?
- **What was the worst decision, and what pushed you to it?** Was it external pressure, or did you follow a misguided hunch?

Reflecting on these can guide you to make future decisions that are more aligned with who you truly are. Additionally, you'll be far happier with your decisions when you make decisions that get you in touch with your inner voice and divine intelligence using the takeaways from above.

Finding Your Purpose Beyond the Paycheck

Remember, your purpose doesn't have to be tied to your job. For some, purpose is found in art, in family, in adventure, or in service to others— it's all about what fills your cup. It's crucial to weave your purpose into your everyday life to truly enrich your existence.

If you're scratching your head wondering what your purpose might be, ask yourself: *What would I do if money and time were no object?* Let that guide your thoughts.

Creating Your Purposeful Path

Once you've got a handle on what makes your heart sing, it's time to lay out some potential paths. Maybe you're considering a career shift, diving into a new relationship, or overhauling your health routine. Whatever it is, let's break it down:

Mapping Out Your Pathways

Consider three different life paths you could take from here. For each, jot down what you foresee as the positives and negatives. This isn't just about dreaming—it's about strategically planning your next moves based on real, heartfelt goals.

Pathway 1:

- Positives: List the benefits and upsides.
- Negatives: Note potential drawbacks and risks.

Pathway 2:

- Positives: What good could come from this choice?
- Negatives: Are there elements that might not align with your deepest desires?

Pathway 3:

- Positives: How could this path enrich your life?
- Negatives: What are the possible challenges or misalignments?

Reflect and Decide:

Sum up the positives and negatives, weigh them carefully, and decide which path feels not just right but resonant.

Embracing Lifelong Wellness

Remember that regardless of what life path you choose, the *Wellness Unfu*ked* journey isn't a sprint; it's a marathon without a finish line. Wellness evolves and adapts over your lifetime. It's about finding balance and adjusting as your needs and circumstances change. While it's crucial to stay committed, it's equally important to be flexible and kind to yourself when life throws curveballs.

As you reflect on your journey, use this moment to also project forward:

- What are the next milestones you aim to achieve?
- How will these efforts blend into your long-term vision for health, happiness, and success?

Consider the broad spectrum of your life's timeline, from birth to the present, and imagine extending that line into the future:

- Where do you see yourself in the years to come?
- How do the steps you're taking now help you move toward that vision?

Let's get started & map out your *Wellness Unfu*ked Timeline* to reflect all of your past, current, and future *Wellness Unfu*ked* milestones.

Grab a pen and paper, or use a digital software that allows you to create curvy lines and text. At the top of your sheet, write, *"My Wellness Unfu*ked Timeline."*

Next, draw a curved line that is the timeline of your life, and fill in your *Wellness Unfu*ked* milestones. Begin by adding in the milestones of your past that have brought you to where you are now.

Now, write down your wildest dreams for your body, mind, spirit, and life.

As an example, I have included the *Wellness Unfu*ked* Timeline for Samuel, the Business Entrepreneur.

My Wellness Unfu*ked Timeline

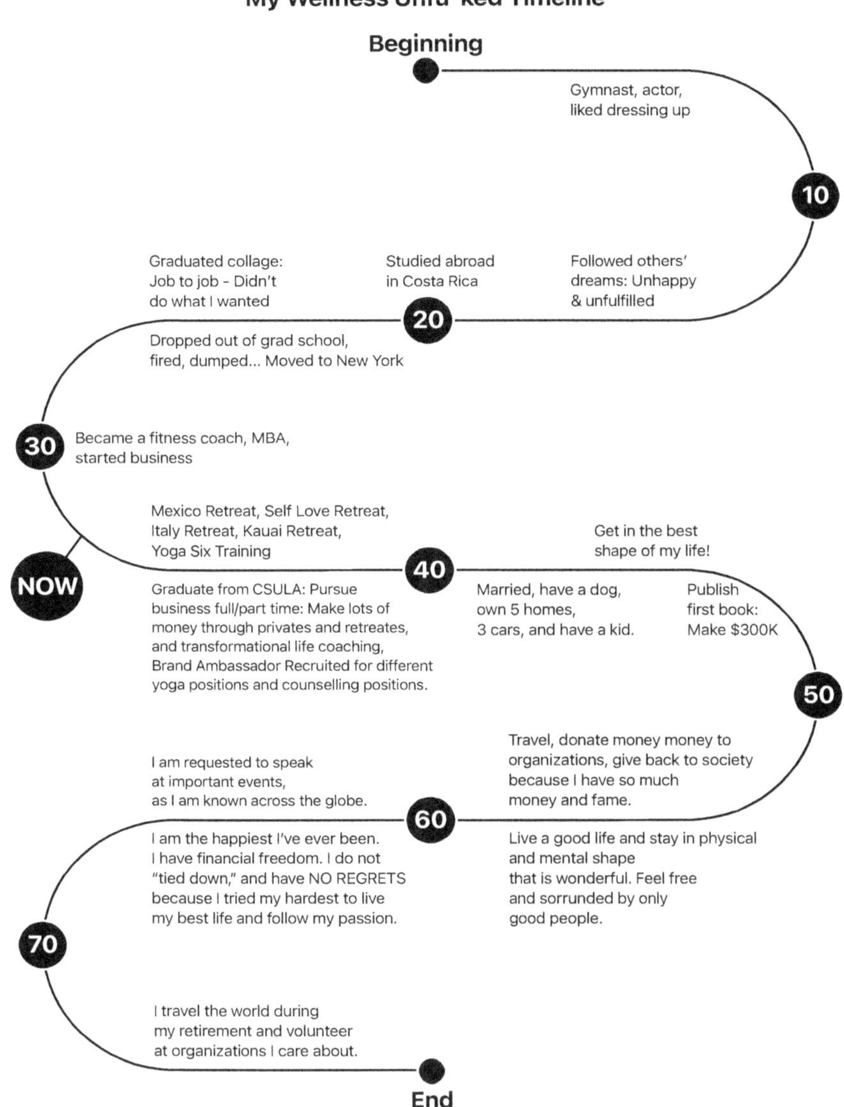

Your *Wellness Unfu*ked* Timeline will assist you in both celebrating all that you've already achieved and deciding what you're calling in during the next weeks, months, and years of your amazing life. And just the act of writing down your goals already makes them more likely to happen. Keep in mind that taking inspired and aligned action is key to manifesting your desires!

SECTION 6:

MANIFESTATION AND YOUR INNER KNOWING - THE SPIRITUAL PILLAR

CHAPTER 16

CONNECTING WITH SPIRITUALITY - INNER GUIDANCE AND WISDOM

Welcome to a chapter that dives deep into the spiritual waters of your life! If there's one thing those living joyful, fulfilled lives have in common, it's a vibrant spiritual practice. Whether it's rocking out in a religious service, meditating in nature, or simply sitting quietly with your own thoughts, spirituality is a game-changer. It provides not just a refuge in times of storm but also a beautiful space for celebrating the good times.

For those who might not vibe with traditional religious paths, spirituality still offers a rich tapestry of experiences. Think of it as the stained glass window of life, each pane a different color, each reflecting its unique light. It's about finding what lights up your soul, giving you strength and community when you need it most, and a place to soar when you're ready to fly.

Daily Spiritual Practices to Connect and Reflect:

1. **Morning Alignments**: Start your day by connecting with the universe. Whether it's prayer, meditation, or writing out your intentions, make it a sacred ritual.

2. **Community Connections**: If you're drawn to group energy, explore spiritual communities that resonate with your beliefs. Dive into their practices, attend services, or join group meditations. Make sure their values uplift and support who you

are, especially if you're part of an LGBTQ+ family like me—I
never compromise on love and acceptance.

3. **Nature's Nurture**: Never underestimate the power of a quiet
   walk in the park, a hike in the hills, or a lazy hour by the sea.
   Nature reconnects us to the essence of who we are beyond the
   hustle and bustle.

In the space below, journal your thoughts on how you currently connect
with your spirituality. What practices resonate with you? What steps will
you take to deepen these connections?

CHAPTER 17

UNLEASH YOUR INNER POWER – MANIFESTATION AND INTUITION

In this era of unprecedented distractions, the greatest challenge often lies not in the external world but in our ability to tune inwards and listen to our inner wisdom. The answers to our deepest yearnings and life's questions are nestled within us.

Yet, in a world where the average millennial is projected to spend around 11 years engrossed in their smartphone, it's no surprise that many of us struggle to hear our own voices amid the constant buzz of notifications, likes, and virtual interactions.

Through taking the steps outlined in these next pages, I began manifesting *with intention*. Instead of making everyone else's priorities my own, I decided what I truly wanted rather than what society deemed was "successful."

Next, I attracted, rather than forced, love, health, wealth, and happiness into my life. And most importantly, I continued to enjoy this process, even when things didn't work out as planned.

Now, let's begin! Get ready to magnetize bountiful love, health, happiness, and success, even in today's busy world.

Harnessing the Power of Intention and Manifestation

To access and activate our greatest potential for long-term success and fulfillment, begin by quieting the noise and focusing inwardly. Spend some time in complete silence and reflect on what would make you truly fulfilled as you manifest your desires.

This step is incredibly important, as actions motivated by negative emotions or driven by ego can lead to a fleeting, hollow type of success that often spirals into dissatisfaction or worse.

Setting aside time daily for meditation and journaling is crucial—be it 15 to 30 minutes. These practices help realign our actions with our highest selves and clarify our true purposes.

Trusting Your Intuition

Your intuition is a potent compass that navigates you through life's storms to your greatest destinations—purpose, love, and optimal health.

But to truly harness this power, you must create sanctuaries of silence in your day. Take breaks for your mind and body to recover and reconnect, even if it is just a few minutes between tasks.

And also, remember to continue disconnecting from social media after 9 p.m. and before the morning rush. This practice gives your mind the space to acclimate to your true environment, free from the digital world's distortions.

Practical Exercises for Manifestation

Now that you've created time for reflection and connection, let's change your energy to change your life!

Manifestation begins with the profound act of feeling the reality of your desires in the present moment:

- If you yearn for love, start by cultivating a deep love for yourself today.
- If health is your goal, celebrate and cherish your body's capabilities and strengths right now.
- If you seek wealth, embody the mindset and habits of abundance immediately.

This process involves three powerful steps:

1. **Be It**: Embody the qualities of the person who already possesses your desires.
2. **Do It**: Take actions that a person with your desired achievements would take.
3. **Have It**: Prepare to receive and welcome the success that will surely come.

If you desire to attract love into your life, it's time to love yourself radically. This first means transforming how you think about yourself through self-loving affirmations, actions, and thoughts. Next, begin dating yourself. Take actions to help you feel good now, like going on a self-love date, treating yourself to an exciting solo trip, or doing a photo shoot with just yourself.

The third step of manifestation—when your dream partner magically appears—occurs magically when your energy is in complete alignment with what you're attracting, you're in the present moment, and you are taking aligned actions.

Remember that the "how" of your manifestation is unknown. If you're attracting love, for example, you could meet your dream partner on a dating app or countless unexpected places like your social media DMs, the grocery store, or through your hair stylist.

To speed up this beautiful process of manifestation, take actions that feel good while anchoring in the present moment.

Transformation takes place in the here and now.

And I don't want you to miss out on the train of success that sometimes only comes once in a blue moon!

To level up even higher in your manifesting abilities, become a creator more than a mere consumer on social media. This means actively contributing, sharing, and engaging in ways that feed your soul and amplify your voice rather than passively scrolling. And when you do engage, let it be intentional, curating content that uplifts and inspires both you and your audience.

Taking aligned actions while being beautifully vulnerable will increase your chances of magnetizing your desires sooner.

And keep in mind that the energy that you put out there is received back in beautiful, novel ways.

Get ready for love, health, and wealth to come to you rather than you having to chase them down!

Manifesting with Intention

Finally, to anchor your intentions in the physical world, engage in daily affirmations and visualization exercises. Breathe in your desires deeply, feel them coursing through your veins, and then act—with joy and conviction—on those inspired impulses that drive you *toward* your goals. This isn't just about achieving what you want; it's about becoming who you are meant to be.

So, let's start now. Breathe in your desire, feel it now, and exhale any negativity!

Let's harness the power of your intentions and step boldly into a life where your inner wisdom and manifesting power create a reality that is not only successful but deeply fulfilling.

This is your time to shine, to manifest your desires, true purpose, and your highest potential.

Manifesting with Intention & Gratitude: Unleashing Your Manifesting Power

Gratitude is not just a practice—it's the highest frequency at which you can resonate. When you actively appreciate what you already have, you create a magnet for more. Every moment of gratitude sends a powerful signal into the universe, echoing, "More of this, please!" Conversely, dwelling on lack or frustrations only multiplies them. So, by cherishing the good now, you pave the way for abundance in relationships, health, and joy.

Pause for a moment, right here. Close your eyes and think deeply about what you are grateful for. Inhale deeply . . . now exhale slowly. How does that feel? That warmth, that light inside you—that's your spirit dancing at a high vibration.

Intention is your secret ingredient, the catalyst for manifesting your desires. Your intention is what you give in exchange for your desires without the expectation of receiving anything in return. When you intend to give back, the universe responds profoundly to this generosity of spirit.

For me, sharing my journey—be it through exuberant dance videos, insightful podcast episodes, or motivating posts—has not only enriched the lives of others but also brought unexpected blessings back to me tenfold. This synergy of giving and receiving has propelled my mission with Fitergy, where we offer premier lifestyle consulting that transforms bodies, minds, and lives.

Now, let's begin manifesting with intention!

As an example, check out the following *Unfu*ked Gratitude & Intentions Journal* for James, the life coach who is manifesting success, love, and amazing health.

My Intention: I intend to give back to others through sharing positivity and wisdom in my email newsletter, social media outlets, and in-person events and interactions. I will facilitate life-changing coaching programs personalized to my clients' goals while calling in my dream partner.

Gratitude Journal:

- I am grateful for my wonderful roommate, dog, and safe place to live.
- I am grateful that I have 7 clients.
- I am grateful that I have $4,000 in savings and $50,000 in retirement and investments.
- I am grateful for my good looks, charisma, and sense of humor.

- I am grateful that I went on a trip to Mexico last spring.
- I am grateful for my ability to run, exercise, and play tennis.
- I am grateful for my mom, sister, and friends.
- I am grateful that I can pay my rent and monthly expenses.
- I am grateful that I went to my friend's wedding and had a blast!
- I am grateful for my unique, sexy personality.

Now, I invite you to dive into the *Unfu*ked Intentions & Gratitude Journal* in the appendices. Ensure that your intention aligns both with what you enjoy doing and feels good. And remember to create affirmations that feel good and illuminate what you have to be thankful for now.

As you jot down your thoughts, let positivity flow through you. Then, record these powerful affirmations and intentions on your device. Make listening to them part of your morning ritual to supercharge your day and manifest your dreams with precision and passion.

Let's harness the magic of gratitude and intention together. Start transforming energy into action, and action into a spectacularly unfu*ked reality!

SECTION 7:

ENJOY - YOUR WELLNESS UNFU*KED JOURNEY

ENJOY YOUR UNFU*KED WELLNESS

As we reach this transformative point in your journey, it's crucial to pause and reflect. Reflecting on your progress not only highlights how far you've come but also aligns your actions with your deepest aspirations. This is a common practice among successful individuals and organizations—they don't just set goals at the beginning of the year; they continuously evaluate their progress.

Take a moment to consider:

- **What's been going well?** Celebrate these wins, no matter how small.
- **What challenges are you facing?** Identifying these helps you pivot your strategies more effectively.
- **How will you refine your approach over the next week?** Small tweaks can lead to significant results.

Celebrating Achievements and Milestones

Every step forward deserves recognition. When you acknowledge and celebrate your progress, you reinforce the behaviors that got you there, making it more likely you'll maintain this momentum. Reward yourself with experiences that resonate with the new you—whether it's a quiet evening with a book, a lively dinner with friends, or a peaceful walk in nature. These moments of joy not only uplift your spirit but also attract more positive outcomes into your life.

Here's how you might plan a rewarding self-love date:

- Choose an activity that fills you with joy and peace.
- Make it a regular part of your schedule to continuously celebrate your growth.

What self-love date would fill your cup? Plan it and schedule it for some time in the next seven days.

And even before you call in your dream body, mind, and life, it's critical to celebrate how far you've come by treating yourself to something even greater, whether it be a retreat, massage, or even a music concert with one of your favorite artists.

What's one thing that you want to do before you transition out of your body?

Schedule this activity into your calendar sometime within the next year. You can even time this activity in alignment with your *Wellness Unfu*ked* challenge as a reward for all of your hard work and determination!

CHAPTER 19

THE WELLNESS WARRIOR'S TOOLKIT - RESOURCES FOR CONTINUED GROWTH

To ensure your growth never stagnates, it's essential to have a toolkit at your disposal filled with resources that keep you inspired and on track. This includes books, apps, and digital communities that support your wellness journey.

Essential Tools for Ongoing Development:

- Presence: Meditate & Thrive App: Start your day with guided meditations.
- Insight Timer App: Customize your meditation experience with a variety of background sounds and durations.
- My Fitness Pal App: Monitor your nutritional intake and physical activity to ensure you're on track.
- Renpho App: Track your body's changes, celebrating both muscle gains and fat loss.

To maintain this momentum, engage with people in person and online who inspire and motivate you. Connect with me on social media platforms like Instagram, Facebook, and LinkedIn, where I share daily insights and encouragement. Join our thriving Facebook community to share your journey and learn from others who are on similar paths.

Keep in mind that *this book* is always available for quick reference as you manifest your dream body, mind, and life. Maintain it and your reflections close at hand so that you can easily reference your takeaways, action steps, and coping tools for future reference.

SECTION 8:

TAKE ACTION - YOUR WELLNESS UNFU*KED REVOLUTION BEGINS NOW

CHAPTER 20

THE *WELLNESS UNFU*KED* CHALLENGE

Are you ready to truly transform your lifestyle and identity? Let's embark on a 30-day *Wellness Unfu*ked* Challenge. Select an aspect of wellness to focus on each day, ensuring to incorporate rest days to maintain sustainability.

Setting Up Your Challenge:

- Decide which of the Four Pillars of You (Mind, Body, Spirit, and Life) you'll focus on and why.
- Plan daily activities that reflect your chosen pillar, gradually increasing in intensity but allowing for adequate rest.

This challenge allows for not only personal growth but also the development of community and sharing. Document your progress and share your experiences in our Facebook group or via email. This visibility not only keeps you accountable but also inspires others to join you in this life-changing journey.

Now, take a few moments to journal your initial thoughts as you prepare to start this challenge. What are your expectations? What do you hope to achieve? Write it all down and step boldly into this new phase of your wellness journey. Together, let's celebrate the unfu*ked, unfiltered, and unstoppable you.

***Wellness Unfu*ked* Challenge**

Tips:

- Begin with small, easy actions, and slowly increase the intensity
- Include breaks
- Place this challenge somewhere that you can see it every day in order to increase your likelihood of success

My *Wellness Unfu*ked* Goal: ______________________________

1	2	3	4	5
6	7	8	9	10
11	12	13	14	15
16	17	18	19	20
21`	22	23	24	25
26	27	28	29	30

Now that you've mapped out your 30-day *Wellness Unfu*ked* Challenge, it's crucial to not only celebrate your progress but also to strategize for the inevitable bumps along the way.

Albert Einstein famously said, "Life is like riding a bicycle. To keep your balance, you must keep moving." This metaphor beautifully captures the essence of navigating life's unpredictability.

It's in the troughs of our journeys where we often gain the most insight and achieve the most growth. The key is how we respond to the unexpected challenges we encounter along our paths to health, love, and healing.

Staying Resilient and Preparing for Setbacks

In the face of adversity, it's vital to have a support system, use self-kindness affirmations, and harness the power of resilience to adapt and adjust your strategies as necessary.

Remember, every setback is an opportunity to refine and strengthen your approach.

Additionally, mental health counseling can be a powerful ally in your wellness toolkit. The World Health Organization highlights mental and substance use disorders as leading causes of disability worldwide. Recognizing signs of mental health issues—such as changes in mood, thought patterns, behaviors, a sense of disconnection, or reliance on unhealthy coping mechanisms—is crucial.

On my journey, I underwent two years of therapy as part of my Master's in Counseling program. This experience was transformative, as it equipped me with the tools to thrive in health, wealth, and love, inspired me to pursue further training in yoga and personal training, and also served as the foundation for my ongoing coaching service and founding both Luke Yoga & Fitergy.

Evaluating Your Mental Health Needs

Now, take a moment to reflect:

- Are there signs that you might benefit from professional mental health support?
- How do you currently maintain your mental wellness, ensuring it receives as much attention as your physical health?

Reflecting on Your Journey

"Life is only a reflection of what we allow ourselves to see." – Trudy Symeonakis Vesotsky

Now that you've taken action toward your desires through *Wellness Unfu*ked*, it's critical to reflect on your greatest takeaways as you continue forward fearlessly.

During your *Wellness Unfu*ked* journey, you have made some profound shifts in where you're going, what you're doing, and how you're feeling. All of the answers are within you now.

With this in mind, let's connect with your inner voice and reflect on how far you've come, the opportunity that you see now, and where you're going. As we draw near the end of this book, I invite you to deeply reflect on your entire *Wellness Unfu*ked* journey:

- What have you gained from these experiences?
- What have you had to let go of?
- What direction is your path taking you next?

My Wellness Unfu*ked Reflection

Use the space below to jot down your thoughts, feelings, and insights. Reflect on your greatest achievements, the obstacles you've overcome, and the lessons you've learned. It's time to celebrate your journey and make a blueprint for continuing your path to unfu*ked wellness.

By documenting your experiences and insights, you not only acknowledge your growth but also set the stage for the next chapters of your life. Keep moving forward, keep balancing, and remember, every pedal stroke takes you closer to the ultimate vision of your best self. Let's celebrate the journey, embrace the lessons, and continue to strive for a life that's not just lived but passionately loved.

Connect and Grow with the Community

Congratulations on completing *Wellness Unfu*ked: Rewrite Your Story, Reclaim Your Life!* Through hypnosis, energy and nutritional medicine, movement, and so much more, you are now reprogramming your body, mind, emotions, and life for your unique definition of success.

Now that you've completed this practical guide to lifelong happiness and purposeful living, get ready for deep, meaningful change in your health, relationships, and self-perception.

And together, we are stronger!

To amplify your journey and connect with like minds, let's connect on:

- **Facebook**: Join our vibrant community here.
- **Instagram**: Follow @limitless_luke for daily inspiration.
- ***Wellness Unfu*ked* Course Website**: Enroll now for **bonus resources & worksheets** at wellness.fitergy.co.
- **TikTok**: Dive into quick wellness tips with @lukelintott.
- **YouTube**: Subscribe to live your best life: https://www.youtube.com/@LukeLintott.
- **LinkedIn:** Join my network on LinkedIn for professional growth and wellness updates.
- **My Podcast**: Lifestyle with Luke Lintott.
- **Email**: Reach out for direct guidance at lukelintott@gmail.com.

Thank you for sharing *Wellness Unfu*ked* with those who bring you higher.

And if this book positively impacted your existence, thank you kindly for your review.

Let's get *Wellness Unfu*ked* to go viral, resulting in a healthy, harmonious, and peaceful world.

As we wrap up this transformative ride, I'm not bidding you farewell; I'm stepping beside you as we continue to unfu*k our wellness. I am immensely proud to be part of your journey toward a vibrant, unfettered life.

With all my heart, radical blessings, and a toast to our enduring health and love,

Luke Lintott, M.S. (he/him/his)
Lifestyle Consultant
CEO & Founder, <u>Fitergy</u> & <u>Luke Yoga</u>

SECTION 9:

BONUS CONTENT - YOUR WELLNESS UNFU*KED EXPANSION KIT

COMPREHENSIVE TOOLS AND INSPIRATIONS

Unlock your fullest potential with these worksheets, checklists, and exploration tools—all carefully designed to ensure your journey through wellness is transformative and thoroughly unfu*ked.

Unfu*ked Affirmations Worksheet

- **Record**: Input these affirmations into your device for daily reinforcement.
- **Display**: Place them where you'll see them often—think bathroom mirrors, bedroom walls, or as smartphone wallpapers.
- **Internalize:** Use the hypnosis track available through the Wellness Unfu*ked Course Website to deeply embed these affirmations into your subconscious at wellness.fitergy.co.

Letter From My 120-Year-Old Self

- Envision: Write a letter from your future self filled with wisdom, gratitude, and insights from a well-lived life, then record it to revisit every morning.

Unfu*ked Visualization Script

- Record and Replay: Capture your visions in your own voice, and make listening to them part of your morning ritual.
- Script Start: Each script begins powerfully with "I am so excited for…"
- Use the hypnosis track available through the *Wellness Unfu*ked Course Website* at wellness.fitergy.co to deeply embed these affirmations into your subconscious.

Unfu*ked Intentions and Gratitude Journal

- Record Your Progress: Keep a digital or physical journal that not only tracks your intentions but also what you are grateful for right now.

Unfu*ked Morning Ritual

- **Wake Up Invigorated**: Start with a tablespoon of vinegar mixed in water.
- **Empower with Audio:** Listen to your Unfu*ked Affirmations, Visualization Script, Letter From My 120-Year-Old Self, and the day's Intentions & Gratitude.
- **Meditate**: Dedicate at least 6 minutes to meditation using the Presence: Meditate & Thrive App, Insight Timer App, or enjoy the silence. Screen time and social media can begin one hour after rising.

Unfu*ked Evening Ritual

- **Disconnect to Reconnect**: Power down and step away from all screens and social media at least one hour before bedtime to clear your mental space.
- **Meditation/Hypnosis**: Engage in a calming meditation or hypnosis session from my YouTube channel and the *Wellness Unfu*ked* Course Website, or simply embrace the tranquility of silence to prepare your mind for rest.
- **Unwind Your Way**: Spend the final moments of your day doing something you love, whether it's losing yourself in a good book, the meditative rhythm of knitting, or reflecting through journaling.

Embrace this evening ritual to nurture your spirit, calm your mind, and ensure every night leads to a more refreshed and unfu*ked tomorrow.

***Wellness Unfu*ked* Detox Program Checklist**

- **Morning Kickstart**: Begin with half a lemon squeezed into water, followed by fresh celery juice.

- **Evening Wind Down**: Enjoy a soothing cup of Chaga, Hibiscus, or Lemon tea.
- **Continuous Cleanse**: Daily detox from common disruptors like sugar, flour, and processed foods.

Detox Food Journal & Reflections

Map out your 9-day detox journey with structured daily entries to reflect on your dietary choices and their impacts on your wellness.

Day 1

Day 2

Day 3

Day 4

Day 5

Day 6

Day 7

Day 8

Day 9

Wellness Unfu*ked Recommended Readings

Embarking on your journey through _Wellness Unfu*ked_ has hopefully ignited a passion for further exploration into wellness, self-love, and transformation. As you continue to cultivate a life filled with health, wealth, and joy, these carefully selected books are resources that I have found deeply impactful in my own journey. They complement and deepen the principles you've encountered here, each offering unique insights and practical tools to enhance your path to unfu*ked wellness.

1. **_Good Vibes, Good Life_ by Vex King**
   - Dive into this transformative book to discover the art of radical self-love and unlock your inner potential. Vex King's insights have inspired me to embrace positivity and significantly influenced the development of key concepts in this book.

2. **_Practical Law of Attraction_ by Victoria Gallagher**
   - For those ready to manifest their dreams into reality, this guide demystifies the Law of Attraction. Victoria's structured approach offers clear, actionable steps that complement the manifestation techniques discussed in _Wellness Unfu*ked_.

3. **_Medical Medium Cleanse_ to Heal by Anthony William**
   - Anthony William provides groundbreaking insights into cleanse-based healing. This book has been instrumental in shaping my understanding of gut health and its role in overall wellness. It offers recipes and cleanses that align with the detox strategies we've explored.

4. ***The Self Love Workbook by* Shainna Ali**

   - Embark on a journey of self-discovery and healing with Shainna Ali's workbook. It's a practical tool that has enriched my practices around self-esteem and happiness, echoing the self-love principles that are foundational to *Wellness Unfu*ked*.

Each of these authors has contributed to the wellness landscape in significant ways, guiding not only my personal transformation but also enriching the content and strategies I've shared with you. As you explore these readings, you'll gain further insights and tools that will support your journey to a vibrant, unfu*ked life.

ACKNOWLEDGMENTS

In the journey of life, we encounter many guides—some light our path, while others challenge us to grow beyond our imagined limits. I am deeply grateful for the myriad of mentors, teachers, and wise souls who have inspired me to chase my dreams. People like Jorge Cruise, Asa Leveaux, and Emily Sussell have not only been incredible sources of knowledge but also pillars of support in my personal and professional growth.

Equally, I must acknowledge the invaluable lessons learned from challenging relationships and the complex systems around us. These experiences have molded me into the resilient and determined individual I am today. They've taught me the value of strength in adversity and the power of transformation through persistence.

To my friends and family, your unwavering support has been priceless. Your belief in my vision has fueled my journey through every high and low.

And to my incredible clients, thank you for entrusting me to help you reach your transformation goals. Your courage and commitment to change inspire me every day.

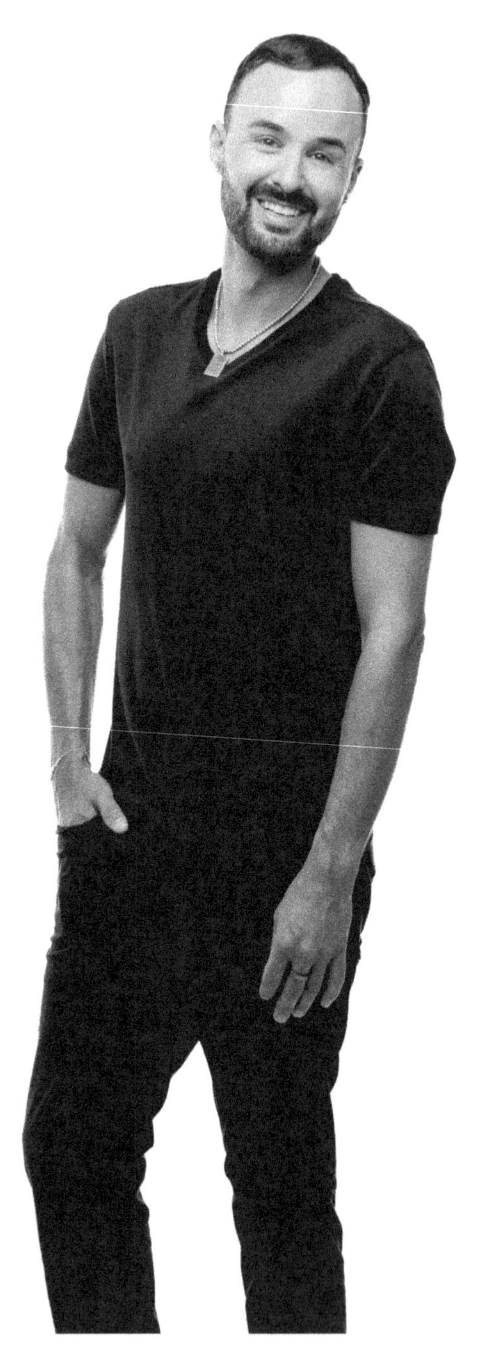

ABOUT THE AUTHOR

Luke Lintott, M.S., PPS, stands at the vanguard of health and wellness, embodying the role of a certified counselor, personal trainer, yoga teacher, and Lifestyle Consultant. As the visionary founder and CEO of Fitergy & Luke Yoga based in San Diego, CA, Luke is dedicated to elevating human potential through holistic approaches to wellness.

His expertise spans mindset enhancement, physical fitness, self-love advocacy, and lifestyle optimization. With a strengths-based methodology, Luke empowers his clients to achieve health, happiness, and holistic success. His work promotes not only personal well-being but also financial prosperity through innovative wellness programs.

Luke's passion for inclusive and transformative wellness extends beyond personal sessions to life-altering retreats, dynamic public speaking engagements, and his popular podcast, "Lifestyle with Luke Lintott." Whether on the mat, in a workshop, or through the airwaves, Luke's commitment to making wellness accessible and transformative for all resonates deeply within the global wellness community. His efforts continuously aim to break down barriers and promote a more inclusive environment where every individual has the opportunity to thrive.

Learn more at lukelintott.com and connect with Luke on Instagram at @limitless_luke.

www.ingramcontent.com/pod-product-compliance
Lightning Source LLC
Chambersburg PA
CBHW071435130726
47997CB00006B/2090